Shostakovich

Shostakovich

N.V. Lukyanova

Translated by Yu. Shirokov

PAGANINIANA PUBLICATIONS, INC.
211 W. Sylvania Avenue, Neptune City, N. J. 07753

Contents

Dmitry Shostakovich.

A NOTE TO READERS

This is a book about Dmitry Shostakovich, one of this century's greatest composers—about his life and art and the importance of his compositions. For decades, his music has been heard in concert halls and opera houses throughout the world. Its superlative artistic merits and noble moral appeal invariably evoke the admiration of vast audiences. Over the last 50-odd years, scores of monographs and hundreds of articles about Shostakovich have been published. Each of them—be it a special research paper or a book for the general public—is filled with infinite respect for the genius and the immortal truth of his music.

In 1921, when Dmitry Shostakovich's name first appeared in the newspaper *Zhizn Iskusstva* [*The Life of Art*] along with the names of other young musicians, the reporter could hardly have foreseen Shostakovich's significance in the history of world music. Nevertheless, the very mention of his name was significant. Indeed, the young composer would never have caught the public eye, had it not been for that rare keenness of perception and the forceful creative impulse which distinguished all his compositions, even the earliest ones. Years later, in his autobiographical notes, he would call this an "urge to express the essence of life." In all his compositions, whatever their genre, he remained loyal to this lofty principle as long as he lived.

Marietta Shaginyan, a renowned Soviet author, in one of her essays on Shostakovich wrote: "A work of genius lends style to its time." Shostakovich's musical masterpieces are truly flesh-and-blood reflections of our difficult and fascinating time. They bear the imprint of their day, like an eyewitness account, but they are free from the limits of time, as is everything that is part of the treasure of the human spirit. His music is a narrative of a great epoch and is marked by a stroke of genius.

A profoundly patriotic Soviet composer, Shostakovich in art was a citizen of the world, and his art defies national frontiers. At a gathering of good-will envoys from all over the world, he made this impassioned appeal: "Let us help everybody appreciate the beauty of the world. We who speak mankind's common language of art and science, the language of culture, must never tire of bringing this truth home to all—wherever we may live." Shostakovich lived up to his word to the end of his days.

"Every human being is a world in himself, a world which is born and which dies together with him," Goethe remarked once. Indeed, birth and death are the fate of every human being. Great works of art, however, are immune to the law of death. Goethe's poetry and Shostakovich's music live lives of their own. Such is the life of everlasting art. At all times and in every land, however distant, people listening to Dmitry Shostakovich's Fifth or Seventh Symphony, 24 preludes and fugues, or Fifteenth Quartet will say: "This wonderful music was composed by Dmitry Shostakovich. He will never die."

The autumn of 1975 in Moscow was a riot of colors touched with melancholy. The weather was warm; the serene azure of the skies and the transparency of the air delighted the eye. A lazy breeze rustled the treetops along the boulevards, spreading the tang of rotting leaves over the city. Autumn was fading out, slowly shedding its festive garb.

It was a Sunday night on September 14. Smartly dressed couples flocked along Herzen Street towards the Conservatory of Music. Coming to the Smaller Hall, they climbed the stairs to the third floor, exchanging greetings and casual remarks. An elated atmosphere prevailed, as is common at concerts. The season was opening with the Beethoven Violin Quartet performing in the Smaller Hall. Dmitry Shostakovich's Fifteenth Quartet, one of his latest compositions, was on the program.

When the austere rectangle of the stage was flooded with lights, four stern figures stood still at the music-stands, and the instruments seemed to tense in expectation. The oldest member of the quartet, Dmitry Tsiganov, slowly placed his violin on a chair and came up to the edge of the stage. He spoke in a quiet voice almost devoid of emotion, but his words stung the audience with piercing notes of sorrow and pride.

Fifty years earlier, in March 1925, a student quartet of the Moscow Conservatory and a 19-year-old student of the Leningrad Conservatory had met in this hall for the first time. Before long, the quartet won worldwide fame, and the student became a renowned composer. Their hard and enthusiastic work linked the five of them by strong ties of collaboration for the next half century, and the Beethoven Quartet was the first to perform almost all of Shostakovich's chamber pieces. He dedicated two of his quartets to the group and one apiece to each of its members in token of lasting friendship, gratitude and fond remembrance.

Then music filled the hall. Familiar for almost a year, it had been played before in Leningrad and Moscow and praised in the press. The music critics had extolled its harmony and explained its message. On that night, nevertheless, that music seemed to unfold anew.

It was started off by a simple and plaintive violin melody, and then all four voices joined in an unhurried narrative. Every listener heard and felt what was his or her love and hatred, hope and disillusionment, joy and pain. Six movements of music only in a minor key (almost without precedent in world musical history!) passed before the enchanted audience as six chapters of a long and hard human life.

The Elegy (adagio). The Serenade (adagio). The Intermezzo (adagio). The Nocturne (adagio). The Funeral March (adagio molto). The Epilogue (adagio). As the last strains of the Epilogue were slowly dying down, the opening theme of the quartet was suddenly resumed and then sustained.

The wind returns to its course. A new life was being born in the agony of death.

Apprenticeship

THE FAMILY

The past comes to life in the old family album with frayed corners velvety to the touch from long use, in photos on which long decades of time have left a yellowish patina with a fanciful pattern of broken lines. Some of the photos are quite ancient, glued onto hard pieces of cardboard with an inevitable embossed ornament and the studio photographer's name proudly displayed on the back, as was the custom in those days. The faces in the photos are covered with a spiderweb of tiny cracks.

Granddad and Granny: Boleslaw Shostakovich, the son of a veterinary surgeon from Vilno, and Barbara Shaposhnikov, the daughter of the treasurer of Saratov province, first met in Moscow in the 1860s. They were young and boiled with idealistic fervor like all young people of Russia, reading at student parties the works by the revolutionary democrats Chernyshevsky and Herzen, admiring the daring and self-sacrifice of the populist terrorists, and exulting in noble revolutonary ideas. The biographies of the young couple are as scant of detail and as matter-of-fact as the terse lines of the reports, denunciations and verdicts preserved in the secret police archives of His Imperial Majesty's Third Department.

In the general crackdown on dissent that followed Dmitry Karakozov's attempt on the life of Emperor Alexander II, Boleslaw Shostakovich was discovered to be implicated in the escape from jail of the Polish revolutionary Jaroslaw Dombrowski, a participant in the Polish uprising of 1863 who would later rise to prominence as a general of the Paris Commune.

Seized by the secret police, Boleslaw bore up bravely against all the hardships of interrogation and trial. He was found guilty of the crime of "sheltering the state criminal Jaroslaw Dombrowski under the sentence of hard labor and of making forged papers for him." In October 1866, Boleslaw was exiled to Tomsk province in Siberia. He had just turned 20 at the time.

The secret papers supplied to his police escort mentioned the convict's intelligence, presence of mind, talent for organization, and high prestige among his comrades. He was to be kept under round-the-clock police surveillance at the place of exile. Barbara, who had resolutely cast her lot with the revolutionary movement, followed Boleslaw to Siberia of her own free will.

Dmitry Boleslavovich Shostakovich,
the composer's father.

Sofia Vasilyevna Shostakovich (née Kokoulina), the composer's mother.

It is known from family tales, documents and reminiscences that Boleslaw and Barbara did not desist from revolutionary work in exile. They were exposed and deported from Tomsk to Narym, a cheerless, bleak place in the backwoods. Here they taught the ABC's to peasant children and kept a vegetable garden to support their family, which had grown quite large by this time. They had two daughters and four sons. After repeated requests, they were granted permission to resettle in Irkutsk, where they went ahead with their studies to complete their education, did some research, contributed to the local press, and read lectures at the city museum. In time they became well known and highly regarded citizens.

Boleslaw and Barbara tried to give their children the best education they could afford under the circumstances and encouraged their interest in literature, music, and theatrical art. Their son Dmitry went on to study chemical engineering at St. Petersburg University. He graduated with flying colors in 1900. His talent for research was noticed by DmitryI. Mendeleyev, who invited him to work at the Central Chamber of Weights and Measures. The eminent chemist needed young talent.

In the early months of his service, Dmitry showed the intelligence and industry he had inherited from his parents. He was a sociable young man, remarkable for his sound judgment, high moral principles and awareness of his civic duty.

He acclimatized easily in St. Petersburg and before long became popular with his fellow students (as he would later in life with his colleagues), and made many friends and acquaintances. He took a special liking to Sofia Kokoulina, a charming girl with gentle and quiet manners. The daughter of a gold-mine manager in Yakutia, she had been studying the piano at the St. Petersburg Conservatory for a few years, preparing herself for a career as a music teacher.

These two young people immediately found a common language. Both were in love with literature and music, and both had spent their childhood and youth in Siberia. Soon he proposed to her, and in 1902 they received their parents' blessing. The new generation of Shostakoviches had come of age.

At first, however, their life was none too easy. Sofia soon gave up her piano lessons and wholly devoted herself to her family, and her first daughter, Maria. Worse still, try as they would, they could not find a good home, and for a long time they moved from place to place, hauling their books, sheet music and an old Diderichs piano as well as their meager family possessions with them. It was not until the summer of 1906 that they settled at long last at No. 2 Podolsky Street. On September 25, 1906, a son was born to them. They christened him Dmitry in honor of his father.

Three years later, when Dmitry's younger sister, Zoya, was born, their small apartment became too crowded, and soon the family moved to an excellent six-room apartment in House No. 9 on Nikolayevskaya Street where they settled in for a long duration. This house, an ordinary one, has survived and is located near the present-day Moscow Terminal.

The climate in the family was very friendly, and the parents' attitude to their children was even and calm. Sofia skillfully maintained the benevolent atmosphere in the home. They spent their evenings in the sitting room, where the father puffed his cigar and spread the aroma of a cozy home. The children would climb onto their favorite shabby and rickety sofa, taking their toys and books with them. The invariable game leader was Zoya, a mischievous and perky instigator of pranks. Maria meekly and quietly followed her. Dmitry, the boy, was not always infected by the excitement of games and more often silently fussed with some object of interest by himself. The whole family always impatiently waited for springtime when they would again—with merry noise, happy squealing and laughter—move to the country. They longed for picnics in the forest, fascinating games in the open air, and for the coming of a photographer with his big, black box. Photos of those years show the children in a room on Podolskaya Street, the children with a female tutor, the children on an outing with their mother on a river bank.

Their home was famous for its hospitality, and the arrival of guests was always a joyful event. Relatives and friends occasionally came from Siberia and stayed with them for a while. In the dining room, serious and unhurried conversations would go on and on until the small hours. The children often heard such names as Ulyanov (Lenin), Chernyshevsky and Herzen, and *strike, prison* and *Bolshevik* became familiar words to them.

Klavdia Lukashevich, a close friend to Boleslaw and Barbara, was always a source of joyful noise and delightful animation. She was a writer of children's books, who put into them the romantic spirit and the desire for universal happiness and equality. Her books were among the first the Shostakovich children read. Unobtrusively but confidently, she led them into the world of nature and people, taught them to try to be noble and generous, kind-hearted and sensitive. One cannot say today with certainty what was the favorite reading in the home, which books were taken off the bookshelves more often than others, searched for in the heap of sheet music on the piano, or suddenly found in the children's room. But later Shostakovich said that certainly Gogol, Chekhov, Pushkin and Leskov were often read.

> "I began to take music lessons
> at the age of nine. Until then
> I had not felt either an attraction
> to music or a desire to learn it."
> Dmitry Shostakovich: A Life Story.
> June 16, 1926.

Playing music in the Shostakovich home, just as in many other homes of St. Petersburg intellectuals, was a matter of routine in their family life. Dmitry Shostakovich, the father, would readily agree to sing to a guitar accompaniment, and Sofia would sit at the piano for hours. The cellist who lived next door sometimes joined them, and occasionally one or two more people might come over to

Sofia Shostakovich and her children at their country house in Irinovka, near St. Petersburg (1911).

Dmitry Shostakovich at the age of 8.

form a trio or a quartet. They played with joy and
music by Haydn and Mozart, Tchaikovsky and Borodin. W
music began, young Dmitry would silently go about his busine
the children's room or quietly settle beside his mother. He woun
not jump up in delight at the first sounds, nor would he show an
open interest. However, he did love and would always remember
throughout his life the danger and romance of his father's troubled
times as a student and his mother's Conservatory repertoire with
the invariable pieces from Chopin, Liszt and Tchaikovsky. He did
not draw a boundary, and nobody in his family did, between the
classics and the popular genres.

In the meantime, études and scales were already being played in
the home. Sofia gave music lessons to little Maria, and soon, ignoring her son's protests, she began teaching music to him, too. A
good education was inconceivable without music, although no
plans were made in the family to give the children professional
musical training. Mitya, which was the future composer's pet
name, was supposed to have a career in commerce, engineering, ac-
counting or finance.

"My mother insisted that I should begin to learn to play the
piano. I tried to evade that as best I could. In the spring of 1915, I
was at an opera house for the first time in my life. It was *The Tale
of Tsar Saltan* on the stage. I liked the opera, but that did not
lessen my reluctance to study music . . . My mother, however, was
adamant, and in the summer of 1915 I took my first lessons at the
piano under her guidance. We made very good progress. I was
discovered to have absolute pitch and tenacious memory. I quickly
learned musical notation and memorized music by heart without
repetition—it impressed itself on my memory without effort.
Before long, I could read music with facility."

*Dmitry Shostakovich:
Autobiography,* 1927.

The boy's progress was so fast that in a couple of months he was
taken to Ignaty Glyasser's piano courses in a house on Vladimirsky
Avenue, where Maria was already studying. Lessons under an experienced and serious teacher included daily exercises and études
for finger training published in Glyasser's manual "Shakes as the
Basis of Piano Technique," widely circulated at the time. Keen attention was paid to dexterity of movement, elasticity of the fingers,
and the evenness and distinctness of the sounds elicited.
Mathematically precise, cut-and-dried exercises were regarded as a
preliminary stage of training to be followed—invariably in combination with the very same exercises—by the next stage of learning pieces from Tchaikovsky's *Children's Album* and the sonatas of
Clementi, Mozart and Haydn.

Strange as it might seem, the rigid framework of Glyasser's
mechanistic system did not feel like pressure or constraint—at least
outwardly. The boy would confess later that it was a bore to train
under Glyasser. The brother and sister, who were used to diligence
and work on their own, successfully mastered the manual.

After a year, Shostakovich played Haydn and Mozart, and in two years he amazed everybody by his performance of preludes and fugues from *The Well-Tempered Clavier*. It was in the early period of his study at Glyasser's courses that he first felt a gravitation to composition, which at once became steady and irresistible. His mother and father's skeptic irony did not discourage him, nor did Glyasser's. Perhaps his first test of the pen was the piano piece he called "Soldier."

> "Events of the First World War and the February and October Revolutions stirred vehement emotions in our family. Small wonder, therefore, that even what I wrote as a child in those years showed a trend to give vent to my reactions to real life. My first naive attempts at composition were my piano pieces 'Soldier,' 'A Hymn to Freedom' and 'A Funeral March in Memory of Revolutionary Martyrs,' all of which I wrote between the ages of nine and eleven."
>
> (Dmitry Shostakovich "Reflections
> on the Past," *Soviet Music*, 1956, No. 9).

The very titles of these pieces reveal the rebellious spirit and interests of the youthful composer, who imperturbably ignored the good-natured teasing of his near and dear ones.

Shostakovich was born 18 months after Bloody Sunday of January 22, 1905, when tsarist troops massacred a peaceful demonstration of famished people in front of the Winter Palace and 11 years before the October Revolution. The world had not proved to be an orderly place where one could live without a search for clarity. World War I showed its ugly face in the boastful headlines in the newspapers and in the blood and grease on the puttees of crippled soldiers hobbling on the streets. Much of what was going on was unclear, but the boy was keenly sensiive to the throbbing pulse of the time, and for all his youthful naîveté, his urge to express real life in music had already become a compulsion, clear cut and persistent. He grasped the meaning of events in the shaking world with the curiosity of a child, while his memory absorbed with unchildlike tenacity the sounds and colors of those stormy days.

> "I was an eyewitness of the events of the October Revolution. I stood in the huge crowd that listened to Lenin speaking in the square in front of the Finland Terminal on the day he arrived in Petrograd. Although I was very young at the time, that scene engraved itself on my mind forever."
> Dmitry Shostakovich. Excerpt from
> a speech broadcast on October 29, 1960.

The progress of life forcefully introduced changes into the Shostakoviches' plan for the education of their gifted son. Fairly soon it became clear that his instruction in finance at Maria Shidlovskaya's school of business left him no time for training in what had proved a more important subject—music. The boy was transferred to a general school. (Later, when he was a Conservatory

Seven-year-old Dmitry with his sisters Maria and
Zoya at Irinovka.

A 1919 portrait of Shostakovich by the celebrated Russian artist Boris Kustodiev. Inscribed "to my little friend Mitya Shostakovich from the author."

pupil, he would have to change schools again, to the 108th vocational school, which was closest to home). It was also found that Glyasser's method of instruction no longer satisfied Shostakovich, and in the spring of 1918 Sofia took her son to Alexandra Rozanova, her one-time teacher of music and a professor at the Conservatory. In the next 18 months, the way from Nikolayevskaya Street (now Marat Street) to Fontanka Street, where Rozanova lived, became very familiar to the boy.

Rozanova taught her pupils with gentleness and patience, without concentration or exercises, enchanting them with a rich range of shades and nuances. At the most anxious moments of a lesson, she would change over from Russian to a mellifluous and sonorous French. Waiting for a lesson, a student might nestle comfortably in the soft leopard skin in the sitting room, examine the paintings on the walls and the bucolic tapestry on the backs of antique chairs, or simply sit snugly in the warm light near the piano, behind which heavy green curtains hung down to the floor, shutting off the din of street traffic.

The boy was happy to study under Rozanova, and his interest in school subjects was equally enthusiastic. He learned the rudiments of science quickly and without apparent effort, and all his teachers admired his accuracy and industry, pictorial and terse language, and sense of humor.

At school he met Irina and Kirill, the children of the painter Boris Kustodiev. They hit it off immediately. They had very much in common: vivaciousness, a penchant for cracking jokes, yet at the same time a serious cast of mind, and love of music. Music was played quite often at school. Once his two new friends became his partners in an amateur performance of the opera *The Snow Maiden*, in which he played the part of Lel. (For some reason, he refused to sing of how "the cloud whispered to the thunderbolt," although he was thoroughly familiar with Rimsky-Korsakov's music.)

Irina recalled the first time Dmitry visited her family's home:
> "One day . . . after classes, I invited the boy to our home. Mitya Shostakovich, dimunitive and disheveled, handed my father a list of compositions he had learned and sat at the piano. His performance surpassed all our expectations, and Father was simply spellbound by his manner of playing. That day was the beginning of a deep and warm friendship . . ."
> Irina Kustodiev, *Dear Memories*, 1957.

Dmitry Shostakovich's "deep and warm friendship" with the Kustodiev family, which stemmed from their common interest in the theater and music, gave him a new inspiration. He often visited his new friends and, although usually self-conscious and awkward, he felt quite at ease among them. He liked roaming through the rooms, admiring the numerous paintings and sketches of decor designs and of costumes hung on the walls. He would avidly listen to Kustodiev, who easily wandered in conversation from painting to theatrical art to literature. The boy was discovering a new and

...ating world of beauty and suspense. The little pianist was a ...ankful and attentive listener, and the eminent Russian painter sensed and appreciated that. When conversation was drawing to a close, they often exchanged roles, and now Boris Kustodiev was the listener, wise and appreciative. The boy played for him with pleasure, without awkwardness or persuasion, and Kustodiev, a subtle connoisseur of music himself, was one of the first to appreciate the original talent of his young friend.

The circle of friends the Shostakoviches mingled with was steadily widening. In those years, they were frequent guests in the home of Ivan Grekov, a surgeon of citywide renown. His home was a center of attraction for people widely different in age and interests, but all of them talented and fascinating. Among his guests one might meet authors Maxim Gorky (considered the founder of Soviet literature), Alexei Tolstoy (cousin of Leo Tolstoy), Mikhail Zoshchenko, pianist Vladimir Sofronitzky, Konstantin Fedin, and the composer and director of the St. Petersburg Conservatory, Alexander Glazunov. The young Shostakovich had just turned ten at the time, and his mother and father, who were chatting with guests in the sitting room, had no inkling of the brilliant career that lay in store for their son. His playing manner impressed everybody present, and they listened intently as music flowed from under the boy's adroit fingers.

> "Each of the guests felt a surge of emotion when a lean boy in glasses, with thin, pursed lips, a little nose slightly raised at the bridge, absolutely speechlessly crossed the big room . . . and, rising on tiptoe, climbed the seat at the enormous grand piano. By some incomprehensible paradox, the puny little fellow at the piano immediately transformed himself into a daring musician, striking the keys with the force of a man and bringing forth a volcanic eruption of sounds. He played his own compositions brimming with the influences of new music and was so unusually innovative that he made his audience feel as if they were in a theater, where the action on the stage drives the audience to laughter or tears. His music talked and even chattered, at times mischievously. All of a sudden, a confusion of dissonances gave way to a melody that made everybody raise their eyebrows. The boy stood up and shyly retreated to his mother . . . ."
>
> Constantin Fedin, *Gorky Among Us,* 1967.

The pile of sheet music on the Diderichs piano was steadily growing. Over the next three years, the boy persisted in his attempts at composing, and friends advised the Shostakoviches to take him to Glazunov and the Petrograd Conservatory.

> "In the summer of 1919, my parents, impressed by my stubborn efforts in composition, took me to A. K. Glazunov. After I played my pieces for him, he said approvingly that I was on the right track and advised me to enter the Conservatory." *Dmitry Shostakovich: Autobiography,* 1927.

Over the next month, the boy took a crash course in the elementary theory of music and solfeggio. The lessons at the Conservatory were to begin in the autumn.

AT THE CONSERVATORY

For his entrance exams, the young musician, now 13, had prepared a few piano preludes of his own composition. The examination took place, as usual, in Glazunov's office and, according to tradition, was held with much ceremony. The boy's talent was acknowledged by all members of the examining board without exception. His originality clearly showed through in the influences of Alexander Scriabin, Konstantin Liadov and Sergei Prokofiev. He left the director's office as a student of junior courses in two departments simultaneously: composition and pianoforte.

He was enrolled in the composition class under Maximilian Steinberg, a favorite pupil of Rimsky-Korsakov at one time. Steinberg enjoyed great prestige at the Conservatory. He was valued as an excellent professional teacher thoroughly familiar with his subject. A man of honor, he was also highly regarded for his high principles. In April 1905, he made this written statement: "In view of Professor N. A. Rimsky-Korsakov's resignation from the Conservatory, I feel it my duty to quit the Conservatory" which was placed on the director's desk along with hundreds of other similar statements.

In Steinberg's class, the pupils studied in succession all the principal theoretical subjects: harmony, instrumentation, musical form and the theory of composition. A stickler for academic tradition, he led his students through the intricate labyrinths of hard-and-fast rules, restrictions and frameworks. For all that, it was fascinating to study under this stern and pedantic professor, so much so that it would be unfair to rebuke Steinberg for his academicism. In fact, it was the same letter and spirit of the Conservatory and of the entire system of musical instruction that had developed over half a century before. Academicism reigned supreme at the Conservatory, and the subjects taught there were the ABCs of musical knowledge without which the education of a professional composer is inconceivable. Although he was still a youngster, Dmitry Shostakovich realized that quite well, and he would gratefully remember Steinberg's superior professionalism as long as he lived.

> "Everything Steinberg taught me, all his instructions and advice, I avidly absorbed like a sponge. He fostered a good taste in his pupils with great skill and tact. It was from him in the first place that I learned to appreciate and love good music. Steinberg instilled in me admiration for Russian and foreign classics."
>
> Dmitry Shostakovich,
> "Reflections on the Past,"
> *Soviet Music,* 1956, No. 9.

Besides the study of regular subjects, they played a lot of piano duets in Steinberg's class. Shostakovich's phenomenal skill of playing at sight compositions of practically any complexity—from a piano reduction or a score—developed very quickly. They endlessly discussed music by various composers, mostly Russian, with Rimsky-Korsakov topping the list. They analyzed and discussed harmony, form, instrumentation and the finest classical specimens of musical art.

As far as academicism was concerned, Shostakovich the student did not mind it. His fellow students would later recall how skillfully he coped with all the difficulties of the science and art of music and how resolutely and quickly he was building up his own professionalism. This excerpt from Director Glazunov's examination reference shows just how facile the boy was at his studies:

"Shostakovich, Dmitry. Professor Steinberg's class of special harmony. Choral: A; modulation: A minus; oral examination: A plus. Average: A plus.

— A. Glazunov (1920)."

In piano class, Shostakovich continued to study under Alexandra Rozanova, with whose system he was already familiar. His piano technique improved and became more serious, his own manner of execution was now more definite and vivid, and his repertoire was much more complex.

"Shostakovich, Dmitry. Professor Rozanova's piano class. Outstanding musical talent and virtuoso technique. Rendition independent and mature. Excellent sonority. A plus.

— A. Glazunov (1920)."

Always keenly responsive and attentive to the individuality of her pupils, Rozanova herself, however, realized only too well that the talent of Shostakovich required far more than what she could give him. So after a year he went over without much deliberation or hesitation to the class of Leonid Nikolayev, whom he would later describe as "an outstanding pedagogue and a first-rate musician."

In Nikolayev's class, Shostakovich discovered a world he had not known before. Not only a pianist but also a composer by education, Nikolayev keenly sensed the creative spirit of musical performance and cultivated in his students a thorough understanding of the inner logic of a composition. He was intolerant of a superficial attitude to music, however brilliant its performance might be, and his usual comment in such an event would be a curt, "Very nice," and not a word more.

Every lesson Nikolayev gave attracted all his pupils, and they thoroughly prepared for it, providing themselves with sheet music in advance. He who had good luck to be chosen sat at the piano, and while he was playing only the cautious rustle of pages turned disturbed the music. The discussion of the execution was often collective, the least time being devoted to technical faults. Nikolayev justly believed that the performer's desire to convey the artistic conception would at the right instant help him correct the flaws of his execution. The pupil was granted full freedom of initiative and

Ilya Glasser's music class. Twelve-year-old Shostakovich is second right in the front row.

creativity to reveal the message of a composition and convey the composer's idea to the listener.

Shostakovich, who happily combined the talent of a performer and a composer, perfectly fitted Nikolayev's image of the ideal student, who sensed and understood the logical development of a composition "from the inside," so to speak. The boy's progress as a pianist was unusually successful.

> "Shostakovich, Dmitry. Professor Nikolayev's piano class. A musician of outstanding talent with wonderful technique, far above what is normal for his age. His rendition is meaningful and rich in feeling. Forte colors are sometimes insufficient. A plus.
>
> — A. Glazunov (1922)."

The extremely "boring and dry" subject of counterpoint at the Conservatory was taught by the composer Nikolai Sokolov, a lively and cheerful man. The subtleties of polyphony remained as sophisticated as ever, but they were learned without effort under his expert guidance. Sokolov was free from academicism as much as Steinberg was dedicated to it.

Lectures on the history of music, fascinating and interspersed with sudden excursions into the fields of literature, theatrical art, and painting, were read by Alexander Ossovsky, an eminent musicologist and critic, who was protector of the Conservatory. Later Shostakovich would appreciatively recall these lectures.

In the center of all activities at the Conservatory stood the colorful figure of its director, Alexander Glazunov. He knew, understood and helped everybody. He invariably presided over public examinations and quickly wrote down his opinion on examination papers. Fortunately, they have survived in the archives. With unfailing punctuality, he appeared even at examinations of the drummers, which, as a rule, interested nobody at all. He did whatever he could for the benefit of the Conservatory. There was much to be done and this work took up a lot of time and effort.

Glazunov realized that his pupils belonged to a new generation. Though he did not accept all of their ideals, he was happy to see any manifestation of genuine talent among them and admired Shostakovich's brilliant progress.

Lessons on special subjects were given twice a week at the Conservatory. Work after classes more than compensated for the disadvantage of academic isolation and the somewhat narrow framework of regular instruction. The enthusiasm of the pupils was infinite, and there was rich ground for fresh impressions and heated debates.

> "The Conservatory of the period of my youth smelled of cabbage soup and seethed, despite all the hardships of the time, with inspiration. Never before had Russia known such universal thirst for knowledge of beauty and access to art as in the early years of the Revolution with their unprecedented fierce fighting and severe privations." Leo Arnstam, *Music of the Heroic*, 1977.

What were the sources of strength of the young Soviet Republic? Famine struck Petrograd in the autumn of 1918. The bread rations gradually dwindled to an eighth of a pound per day. In the winter, wooden houses were demolished for firewood. Epidemics broke out here and there in the city. But the Republic lived on.

In 1921, the Petrograd Philharmonic opened in the building of the former Noble Assembly. The programs of concerts, most of which were free of charge, were compiled under the personal direction of Anatoly Lunacharsky, People's Commissar for Public Education. Beethoven, Scriabin and other classics were on the repertoire. The new audiences of workers and soldiers and young people longed for heroic music.

In the very first year, a cycle of Beethoven's symphonies was performed in public. The Third, the Fifth and the Ninth symphonies attracted eager crowds. The hall proved too small to accommodate all who had come in the hope of getting in. People crowded between the white marble walls, clustered on the tiers or simply sat on the floor. The enormous crystal chandelier was fogged by the breath of thousands. In an hour it became so hot from the warmth of human bodies that many took off their pea jackets and sheepskin coats. Now and then the audience exploded in a thunder of applause.

At these concerts Shostakovich often saw the awkward, tall figure of a young man listening in fascination or talking and gesticulating excitedly. That was Ivan Sollertinsky, a university student, who would in time rise to prominence as a brilliant lecturer, critic and musicologist. They would become lifelong friends.

Times were still hard for the fledgling Soviet Republic. Russia's former allies, France and Great Britain, were trying to strangle the revolutionary government with the deadly noose of a blockade. Britain was sending lavish arms supplies to the Polish dictator, Józef Pilsudski, for war against Soviet Russia. Capitalist Europe was waiting for the collapse of the Soviets with anticipation. The Republic, however, held its ground.

Little by little, foreign musicians and conductors started coming to Russia for guest performances, at first apprehensively and then with delight. Among them were such celebrities as Oscar Fried, Otto Klemperer, Arthur Schnabel and Egon Petri. They brought along music by Stravinsky, Mahler and Berg, unfamiliar to Soviet audiences.

The people's thirst for knowledge was irresistible. Libraries and clubs, theaters, newspapers and magazines mushroomed throughout the country. Mass theatrical and musical festivals became a matter of course. Their thousands-strong audiences felt their hearts beat in unison with the performers of gala spectacles and concerts, such as *Towards the World Commune* in Petrograd, *Pantomine of the Great Revolution* in Moscow, *The Third of July* in Murmansk, *The Apotheosis of Labor* in Samara—veritable hit parades of revolutionary art of monumental proportions.

The times were matched by the enormous scale of new

developments.

> "My comrades and myself studied musical literature with fascination. We got together regularly, played piano duets and quartets, invited student violinists, cellists and other musicians to join us in forming various companies."
>
> Dmitry Shostakovich, *Reminiscences,* 1962.

There were musical composition clubs to aid regular instruction. One of them united young students of the Conservatory. Serious discussions often broke off with merry laughter, jokes and puns. The students brimmed with the joy of life. Many of the conservatory professors were shocked to see such a merry crowd of youngsters jamming the decorous corridors. In the center of this bantering group were Dmitry Shostakovich, Pavel Waldgart, Leo Arnstam and Pavel Feldt. The violinist Karl Eliasberg, the future conductor of the Leningrad Symphony, stood in the crowd, imperturbable and quiet, time and again burying his face in a score. Bursts of laughter, noise and shouts. These youngsters had no veneration for the venerable walls.

Another circle gathered regularly on Mondays, often over a cup of tea. There were older members here: Vladimir Shcherbachev, Nikolai Strelnikov, Yuri Tyulin, Vladimir Deshevov. Boris Asafiev also came occasionally. They played their own compositions and music not yet familiar to many by Stravinsky, Schönberg, Hindemith and Krenek.

Their assessments might not be always correct: the truth did not reveal itself immediately. But the process of learning one's own self and the world around went on at full speed. Shostakovich's compositions were admired, remembered and quickly circulated in the Conservatory milieu.

On September 27, 1921, Shostakovich's name appeared in the press for the first time, in the newspaper *Zhizn Iskusstva* — the *Life of Art*. Some time later, the press would advance him to the forefront among young composers. But he would all his life try to evade congratulations and praise with his characteristic awkward shyness.

Shostakovich was constantly hard pressed for time. His health was failing, too. Lessons at two departments simultaneously and at the 108th vocational school (he was determined to get a regular secondary education) demanded strict discipline, iron will and hard work. Toward the end of the second year, Shostakovich was on the brink of a nervous and physical breakdown.

On August 16, 1921, Klavdia Lukashevich, the writer of children's books who was a close family friend, wrote to Anatoly Lunarcharsky, People's Commissar for Public Education, on Shostakovich's behalf:

> "Dear Anatoly Vasilyevich,
>
> "In the musical and literary circles, there is much talk about food rations awarded on your instructions to the

most gifted children of Russia . . . I beg your assistance in granting this privilege to the pianist and composer Dmitry Shostakovich, 14 years of age, who is a remarkably gifted boy. At nine years of age, he displayed extraordinary musical talent: phenomenal musical memory, absolute pitch and great knowledge of piano literature. He has already played his own compositions before large audiences . . . The current severe privations and almost constant hunger have had a painful effect on all children, but the plight of such a hard-working and sensitive boy as Dmitry Shostakovich is simply unbearable. Because of chronic undernourishment (he almost never has milk or eggs, meat or sugar, and very seldom has butter), our dear boy is very thin, pale and extremely nervous. And, worst of all, he is developing acute anemia. Now that the chilly Petrograd autumn is not far away, the boy has no good shoes, no rubber overshoes, no warm clothes. We fear for his life. For all their love for him and desire to help, his parents and near ones are unable to give him what he needs to survive and develop his talent . . . In addition to his outstanding musical endowments, the boy has a gentle and noble character, the exalted and candid soul of a child, and is unusually modest . . . His brilliant mind is working tirelessly, to the point of exhaustion . . . His talent cannot thrive without what now matters most—food . . ."

The result: "Award an academic food ration to Dmitry Shostakovich, a pianist and composer, age 14. Signed: A. Lunacharsky."

On February 24, 1922, Dmitry Shostakovich, Sr., died from pneumonia. The attending physician was his friend Ivan Grekov. The bereaved family was left without any means of subsistence. Sofia had to take the job of cashier, and Maria, to give private lessons.

Little by little they adjusted, albeit with difficulty, to their new situation, supporting one another. Sofia strived to help her son to go ahead with his study of music. His health, however, gave way under the stress of constant overwork. A year after his father's death, he developed lymphatic and bronchial tuberculosis. The case was so bad as to require surgical intervention. The doctors insisted that he should go to the Crimea for climatic treatment. The old Diderichs piano had to be sold, and he went south for the summer together with Maria. On their return, he had to search for a job to earn money to repay some of his family's debts. Any job was welcome and as soon as possible. For two years he worked as a pianist playing incidental music for films. Later he would recollect this period as the most feverish one in his life and wasted as far as his art was concerned.

Shostakovich at 17.

The summer this picture was taken, this shy-looking youth completed a symphony that, in the view of many distinguished contemporaries, heralded a new age in music.

His regular duties were as follows: Every evening he sat at the piano in front of the screen and "illustrated" motion pictures with music corresponding to them in "emotion." His Conservatory repertoire and his own compositions were good for the purpose. For those who were not inventive and resourceful enough at this work, special music collections were published: music of passion, music of water, of storm, of fear.

At first he had a very serious, even enthusiastic, attitude to his new job. He tried hard to guess the mood as fast as he could and improvise the right music for what was happening on the screen. Very soon, however, this work began to exhaust him and put his nerves on edge. The quickness of action did not allow a moment of relaxation, and he felt his strength waning with every new session. Digressions from stereotypes were not encouraged and caused misunderstanding, but he hated to present musical cliches of a "desert," of a "quarrel between lovers" as was prescribed in the standard collections. His fee was small and paid irregularly. Once he even had to take his pay grievance to court.

"Then I . . . quit the films, and I haven't been with them ever since. I hope I won't ever have to return there."

Dmitry Shostakovich: *An Autobiography,* 1927.

Shostakovich, however, was mistaken. He would have to come back to the films very soon. It would be in earnest and for a long time.

THE DEBUT

In spite of his illness and surgery, he did not interrupt his study at the Conservatory. He prepared a graduation program for the piano class, a serious program: a prelude and a fugue in C-sharp minor from the first volume of Bach's *Well-Tempered Clavier,* Beethoven's *Sonata No. 21,* Chopin's *Third Ballad,* Mozart's *Variations in C Major,* Schumann's *Humoresque, Venice and Naples* by Liszt and Schumann's Concerto.

> "Shostakovich, Dmitry. Professor Nikolayev's piano class. Richly endowed musical nature. Perfectly mature musician despite his young age. Rendition marked by sincerity and subtle artistic intuition . . . Allowed to take graduation examination.
> Annual average: A plus. Musical maturity: A plus. Public examination: June 28, 1923. Rendition consummate, remarkably simply and sincere. A plus.
> — A. Glazunov."

The examining board had rated Shostakovich's graduation performance at A plus.

It was unnecessary for him to work his way upward to a position of vantage in the performing field. As a pianist, Shostakovich was well known within the musical community, just as were all graduates of Nikolayev's school. The latter's best pupils—Vladimir

Sofronitsky, Maria Yudina and Alexander Kamensky—confidently moved into key positions on the concert stage.

Shostakovich's first public performance upon graduation was held in the Circle of Friends of Chamber Music. Its spectacular success set the stage for his long career as a virtuoso musician.

> "The rendition of the young composer and pianist Dmitry Shostakovich greatly impressed the audience. He played Bach (organ prelude and A-minor fugue in Liszt's paraphrase), Beethoven's *Appassionata,* and his own compositions with that confidence and salience of artistic presentation that distingush a musician who can deeply feel and understand the essence of his art."
>
> – Zhizn Iskusstva *(The Life of Art),* 1923 No. 47

Shostakovich nevertheless continued his lessons under the guidance of Leonid Nikolayev, at first in the latter's home and, after a few months, at the two-year academic course Nikolayev directed at the Conservatory (equivalent to today's post-graduate course). Intensive study of composition in Maximilian Steinberg's class and playing incidental music for films in the evenings (it was not before the beginning of 1926 that he got rid of this job) compelled him to save his strength and use it sparingly if he were to make further progress in the piano.

On November 1, 1925, Shostakovich wrote to Nikolayev.

"Dear Leonid Vladimirovich,

> "I am looking forward to meeting with you one of these days. I wonder when you could receive me for a discussion concerning my studies. I wish to tell you about my studies. I assure you that I am not dwelling, but I am in a fix because of my work in the movie houses. I may be too impressionable, but when I come home from the theater the music rings in my ears, and in my mind's eye I see the film characters I hate. This keeps me from sleeping until 4 or 5 in the morning. I wake up with a headache and in a nasty mood. Ugly thoughts push themselves into my mind—that I have sold myself to the Northwest Film Studios for 134 roubles to become a motion-picture pianist. Then I have to hurry to the Conservatory. Then I come home, have a hasty meal, and off I go to the Splendid Palace again.
>
> "I hope all this will soon be over and I shall be able to study serious piano playing regularly. I have started on Prokofiev's *First Concerto.* Do you approve of my choice? I want to come to you in a few days and get some assignment from you . . ."

In that difficult situation, Shostakovich's exceptional willpower and hard work enabled him to prepare a wide repertoire. Already in July 1926 he left for Kharkov for guest performances with a program that would make an experienced musician envious: Tchaikovsky's *First Piano Concerto;* Liszt's fantasia quasi sonata *Après une lecture du Dante, Funérailles,* the études *Gnomenreigen* and *Waldesrauschen, Canzona, Gondoliere* and *Tarantella* as well as some of his own compositions.

"Dear Leonid Vladimirovich,

"Many thanks for your postcard. I had not expected to hear from you so soon, knowing your reluctance to write letters . . . Apart from Tchaikovsky's *Concerto,* I performed as a solo pianist in Kharkov. On Thursday, July 16, I played my *Klavierabend* there. It took me two days to prepare. I played my own compositions and Liszt. I had great success and was rewarded with a sizeable fee.

"Today I arrived at Anapa, and I am going to rest for a month here. I am very tired after my trip and my performances in Kharkov."

Excerpt from Dmitry Shostakovich's letter to Leonid Nikolayev, July 17, 1926.

Shostakovich went on with his work in composing. In 1923 he sketched his First Symphony. Essential material for it had been collected before and was building up steadily. During his Conservatory years, Shostakovich composed a great deal, more than enough for a student. His first opus was a scherzo for an orchestra, which was followed by the *Theme with Variations* for orchestra, the *Two Krylov Fables* for voice and orchestra, the *Three Fantastic Dances* for piano, the *Suite for Two Pianos* (in memory of his father), another scherzo for the orchestra, the *Piano Trio* and the *Three Pieces for Cello and Piano,* not counting numerous sketches, experimental material and routine study assignments. Jointly with his friends—Gerges Clemenz and Pavel Feldt—he planned to compile a collection of 24 preludes in all tonalities and even wrote some of them.

The *Two Krylov Fables* ("The Dragonfly and the Ant" and "The Ass and the Nightingale") and the *Three Fantastic Dances* became especially popular in the composition community, in the Conservatory and within his close circle of friends. The laconic, outwardly unsophisticated pieces composed by the 16-year-old student suddenly revealed the kind of depth, originality and vividness of creative thinking that are inherent only in talent of unusually wide scope.

"Going back along Korochnaya Street, we . . . took him and Maria to the Vraskys, who lived on Manezhnaya Street. There Dmitry played his *Fantastic Dances* and *Krylov Fables* for us on a wonderful Bluthner piano.

"At last, on that evening, I first heard his rendition of both Liszt and Schumann. I was vividly impressed by his sharp and original creative style.

"Sitting at the piano was a frail teen-ager with a childish profile, but his playing was refined with consummate thought, perfect form and the temperament of a mature maestro. Fantastic images of a grotesque flashed for the first time on that night. With my pale, lyrical timbre, I did not dare to sing the vocal line in the

Krylov Fables. In The Ass and the Nightingale, one could already discern the sarcasm that would become so devastating in his later compositions. The stupid tirades of the Ass could be a sketch for the unsurpassed grotesquery of his early opera *The Nose.* Laconism always requires superior mastery. We listened to piano music but heard orchestral tone colors."

E. Trusova, *Pages of Reminiscences,* 1977.

In 1926 the *Three Fantastic Dances* for piano would be published by the music department of the State Publishing House to become Shostakovich's first composition to have come out in print. On the title page of the edition, he would confidently display his name, "D. Shostakovich, op. 1," as if to acknowledge that of all experiments of his youth this was for the time being the only one worthy of publication. Music critics would praise the *Fantastic Dances* as one of the most interesting works produced by the young composers of the time and promised it a long and happy life. Indeed, it continues to this day.

"The aforesaid pieces are miniatures of fairly lucid piano rendition and a rhythmically clear character. Their melody and harmony are akin to the modern trend of the Medtner-Prokofiev coloration, but in contrast to the Moscow variety of this trend Shostakovich is far more restrained and cautious in selecting his means: he does not shun simplicity and melodic harmony. One can note the superlative piano structure of Shostakovich's music. This quality is particularly valuable now that most piano compositions are but 'some forms in the air.' "

Music and Revolution, 1927, No. 1.

Shostakovich's compositions of the Conservatory period clearly demonstrated distinctive features of his talent: pert and witty scherzos, a collision between contrasting "high" and "low" images and a penchant for pensive, concentrated reflection.

The death of Lenin was a shock to Shostakovich just as it was to the whole country, and the young composer made up his mind to write a large symphony in memory of his country's great leader. He would cope with this theme 30-odd years later, but its tragic and plaintive notes would be audible already in his First Symphony.

In the autumn of 1924, Shostakovich, who often visited Moscow, became involved with a circle of young musicians of the capital. They usually got together in the Oborins' home on Solyanka Street. The most active members were Mikhail Starokadomsky the composer, Lev Oborin the pianist and teacher at the Conservatory, and Vissarion Shebalin the composer. Boris Yavorsky, the pianist and music theorist, was a regular guest. Shostakovich set up more and more contacts, deep, serious and lasting.

"I did not see Dmitry in the summer, because I had gone away shortly before, and now I was glad to meet with him again. He has that remarkable quality that leaves a greater impression after every next meeting, which proves that he is a richly endowed personality. You are lucky to have such a friend."

Excerpt from a letter by Boris Yavorsky to B. Bogdanov-Berezovsky, October 22, 1925.

In the autumn of 1924, Shostakovich made another important acquaintance—Yuri Shaporin—in Leningrad. A recent pupil of Steinberg and Sokolov, Shaporin had looked forward to a meeting with the young composer, of whom he had heard so much from so many, primarily from Glazunov. And he was not disappointed. "We talked on a variety of subjects long into the night. Needless to say, music was also there," Shaporin would say later. Their tastes agreed in many ways, and this similarity bound Steinberg's two pupils by strong ties of common interests. Life would later bring them together for a long time as colleagues working at the Moscow Conservatory. Shaporin would give his comrade solicitous attention, protecting and helping him. In a humorous cartoon drawn by the artist Nikolai Rydlov during the 1930's, Shaporin's powerful torso seems to shield Shostakovich's touchingly frail figure.

"The friendly atmosphere in the Shostakovich family attracted a wide range of people to their home . . . There always seemed to be present friends and acquaintances of all three of the family's young members. This circle of guests steadily widened . . . It began to be joined by colleagues of the young composer, who had caught the public eye, and by people admiring the intellectual climate in his home."

Valerian Bogdanov-Berezovsky, *Adolescence and Youth,* 1966.

On March 20, 1925, a musical soirée was held in the Small Hall of the Moscow Conservatory, with compositions of Dmitry Shostakovich and Vissarion Shebalin on the repertoire. That was the first public concert of chamber music given by either of them. One of Shebalin's compositions was played by what was to become in time the Beethoven Quartet. Shostakovich played his Trio, the *Three Fantastic Dances,* the *Suite for a Piano Duet,* and the *Three Pieces for Cello and Piano.* The audience applauded him half-heartedly out of courtesy but he was certainly not a success. Shebalin was obviously better liked. The setback spurred Shostakovich on, and he completed his First Symphony toward the summer of 1925.

"Shostakovich, Dmitry. Professor Steinberg's class of the theory of composition. Brilliant musical talent. Much fantasy and inventiveness. Currently in a period of quests.

— A. Glazunov."

"Transferred to the class of free composition.

— A. Glazunov (1925)."

Excerpts from Alexander Glazunov's examination references.

Steinberg regarded his pupil's compositions with caution and ambivalence, although he had no specific objections to them. The symphony embarrassed him with something even his keen ear could not grasp. In his diary, on March 8, 1926, Steinberg wrote:

> "Closed meeting of the association. Discussion of Shostakovich's symphony, whose slow movement and labored lyricism I definitely dislike. . . "

The professor confined himself to a comment on a certain rigidity of harmony and orchestration details. The young composer also heard suggestions from Glazunov that the rigidity and uncommonness of musical language be softened here and there.

Shostakovich's First Symphony was accepted as his graduation composition. On April 20, 1926, the Learned Council of the Department of Composition unanimously awarded him a research scholarship.

In the meantime, the Conservatory was in a state of commotion. For the first time in many years, a student's opus was prepared for public performance. Friends in Leningrad and in Moscow were agitated perhaps more than the composer himself.

The premiere was scheduled for May 12, 1926. It was to be performed under the baton of Nikolai Malko, the then-chief conductor of the Leningrad Philharmonic. The program was to be made up exclusively of new works by Soviet composers, and Shostakovich's composition was number one on the list. The full staff and students of the Conservatory were present at his premiere. Glazunov sat in his favorite chair in the sixth row, smiling benevolently and applauding.

> "Nikolai Malko was conducting. At a hardly noticeable motion of the baton, a muted trumpet murmured something amid complete silence. A bassoon responded lazily. Then a clarinet spoke up, followed by a rapid, though not loud, conversation of instruments, each trying to begin its theme all over again. Every new episode revealed Shostakovich as a musician with a cast of mind, character, personality and manner of expression never known before.
>
> "The applause was tumultuous . . . . Many realized that they were witnessing an epoch-making event . . ."
>
> Irakly Andronikov, *The Image of His Music,* 1976.

After the concert, a merry bunch of young people burst out of the Philharmonic Hall onto Nevsky Prospect and as if by tacit agreement, turned their steps to the left, toward Marat Street. It was a chilly May, and a dank wind bit their faces as they went past the bronze horses on the Anichkov Bridge.

In the Shostakoviches' home, the heroes of the occasion—Maximilian Steinberg, Nikolai Malko and of course, Dmitry Shostakovich—were seated at places of honor at the family table. The modest supper was drowned in the cheerful hubbub of voices as the excited guests interrupted one another. Sofia was quiet and happy to see her son's eyes shining from joy. As the conversation went on and on, twilight (or white) nights of May were just beginning in Leningrad; the memorable day of wonderful events seemed reluctant to end.

The party broke up long after midnight. Steinberg and Malko went home by the same route, talking excitedly all along their way down Sadovaya Street. As soon as he came home, Steinberg sat down at his desk and opened his diary, as was his habit of many years, and wrote:

> "May 12. [1926] A rehearsal of the concert in the morning . . . In the evening, the memorable concert. Dmitry's symphony was a spectacular success; the scherzo was played to encores."

The symphony was soon performed in Moscow. In November the graduation composition of a Conservatory student was played for the first time in Berlin under the baton of Bruno Walter.

Well, now he could take a look around. Shostakovich's character had already formed and reached maturity. All who had known him in his youth would point out his most salient traits: reticence, modesty, awkwardness, extreme self-consciousness with a strained gaze behind the thick glasses. He was withdrawn but was also easily amused, lively, witty and sociable. His business qualities were also noticeable to all: persistence, industriousness, concentration on his subject, tenaciousness, and quickness on the uptake as far as innovative ideas were concerned. Paradoxically, nobody sensed in this Conservatory student an open protest against dogma and hard-and-fast rules, a frank defiance of the milieu he had been raised in, one that had constrained Prokofiev so much at the time of his youth.

What embarrassed Steinberg in his pupil's music? Indeed, Shostakovich's compositions had the requisite loyalty to academic tradition and restraint, was based on well-learned school rules and concepts, and a thoroughly planned and clear-cut composition. All the four movements of his symphony were unmistakably in "their right places" in accordance with a time-honored pattern enforced at the Conservatory. The first movement "boiled," as prescribed, with motley colors and diversity of images. The second movement raced along in a swift and vigorous scherzo. The third movement was as lyrical and pensive as a classical model, while the finale returned to stable and dependable convention.

The influences of Scriabin and Wagner, Glazunov and Tchaikovsky were still discernible in this music and, like all Conservatory students, his pupil had not yet avoided the influences of the new "modernistic" music of Stravinsky and Prokofiev, Hindemith and Berg. That was understandable and tolerable to Steinberg, as were the slightly inorganic character of the musical fabric, some far-fetchedness and commonplaces, and flaws in what was otherwise an impeccable orchestration. Such compositions came out of the Conservatory by the dozen, and Shostakovich's symphony also seemed perfectly academic, as if right from a textbook.

For all that, the pupil had excelled the teacher. The first movement "boiled" with imagery, but those images were new, much unlike that to which Steinberg was accustomed. The scherzo sped along, indeed, but at the brisk pace of a gallop, the "low" music of everyday life, and the professor's academically orthodox nature vehemently protested against that. The third movement breathed sincere lyricism, but it was somewhat awkward and inelegant, because the time for new lyricism had not yet come in the world. But to make up for it, the finale seemed comely and well balanced. Yet it was precisely here that the symphony had its weakest points. The time for the right kind of a finale had not yet come either, since much was still incomprehensible in the new world.

The symphony was the living spirit of the times, because it was at the crest of the revolutionary wave sweeping all Russian art. Concepts and judgments were changing, as were images and means, artistic principles and methods, and Shostakovich's symphony heralded innovation that had come to stay. That is why his friends and fellow students welcomed it so enthusiastically and Glazunov applauded so warmly the brilliant musician of the new generation.

"I have the feeling that I have learned a new page in the history of music and met a new great composer."

Excerpt from a letter by Nikolai Malko to L. Izarova, May 12, 1926.

Half a century after his controversial debut, Dmitry Shostakovich — by then a composer acclaimed by the entire world — would stand before an attentive, admiring audience. "The composer must seek contact with his listeners. This is his artistic and moral duty."

Dmitry Shostakovich in 1935.

At A Crossroads

FROM THE FIRST SONATA TO THE SECOND SYMPHONY

On December 12, 1926, the Meyerhold Theater in Moscow gave the first performance of Nikolai Gogol's play *The Inspector General*. On the same day, Shostakovich played his piano sonata, *October*, for the first time in Leningrad. There was the familiar smell of gunpowder in the air around both premieres. Art in the '20s was a battlefield where each army was fighting under its own colors and straining to win. Consensus and indifference were confined to the trains bringing up the rear.

It was a time of heated controversy, in which individual voices sounded too excited at times. Art called into being by that stormy time was not uniform and homogenous, nor did it always reach the summits of aesthetic perfection, for all its passion and sincerity. In its extremes it came to the point of paradox. That paradox was a disease of infancy which would be cured by history itself, and Soviet art, sometimes through short-lived and risky experiments, was groping its way forward.

> "It was by no means easy to understand the aspirations of the young artistic community of those years. These young people deemed it impossible to combine the sensation of novelty of what was going on in life around them with the traditional forms of art. It was a period of enthusiastic quests, of remarkable integrity and of amazing confusion. Often it was not a question of ideas but only of sensations which were for the time being quite vague."
> Grigory Kozintsev, *The Deep Screen*, 1972.

Opinions clashed in everything but the choice of the subject. The victorious revolution longed for an immediate expression in art, and the young Soviet art was therefore searching for new images and techniques worthy of that revolution. The sweeping social change that was in progress called for a reflection in its art of equally great scope and involvement of the masses. The collective was opposed to the individual, and necessity was opposed to the aesthetic and the refined. The old values under this banner were to be resolutely discarded and destroyed. It was only the stern warnings from Lenin and Lunacharsky that restrained the zealots of artistic progress from razing all old art to the ground and "throwing Pushkin overboard from the steamship of modernity."

"We are witnessing a riot of extremes, and hence it is necessary to caution sternly all those who are beginning cultural work for the Republic against excesses. Some individuals believe that any dissemination of 'old' science and 'old' art is pandering to bourgeois tastes, poisoning the young socialist organism with blood from a decomposed old corpse. Extremists obsessed with this delusion are few, but they may cause great harm. To discard science and art on the premise of fighting their bourgeois degeneration would be just as absurd as to demolish on the same premise machinery at factories and railways."

    Anatoly Lunacharsky, *Another Look at Proletcult and Soviet Cultural Work,* 1919.

Thus, opinions concurred only in the choice of subject matter. What followed was a veritable "battle of ideas" wherein the combatants widely diverged in their choice of which path to pursue in art and formed intransigent groups locked in a vehement polemic. Their battlefields were the artistic unions, theoretical art journals, and the daily press.

Some revolutionaries visualized the new art as a simple and austere harmony of glass, electricity and metal. The peasant Russia dreamed of a future invested with a halo of industrialization and spoke up with the voices of Gleb Chumalov in Feodor Gladkov's novel *Cement:* "Years will go by, and the world will shine with the splendor of palaces and mysterious machines . . . It will be a clean realm of glass and tiles, the black, silver and gold luster of diesels, and the gentle, melodious tinkling of levers, hammers and pistons." The music of machines charmed the minds and hearts of enthusiasts of that industrial trend, which would later be called the "constructivism of the '20s."

The new imagery, the new qualities of expression—intensive and rigid lines, clear and forceful rhythms, ceaseless and accurate movements, frank opposition to lyricism—were the most striking in theatrical art and in music. Much of this experimentation with its visible scenery entertains us today by its naively illustrative nature. The echo of the "poetry of metal" was to be heard in the works of the art directors Vsevolod Meyerhold and Sergei Radlov, the choreographers Igor Moiseyev and Leonid Jacobson, the artists Tatiana Bruni and Georgi Yakulov, the composers Vladimir Deshevov and Alexander Mosolov. Even the titles of some composer's opuses had industrial overtones: *A Symphony of Factory Whistles* (Avraamov), *The March of Steel* (Prokofiev), *The Factory* (Mosolov), *Ice and Steel* (Deshevov).

Others imagined the new art as a flourishing poetry of anthems and political agitation, monumental mosaics and frescoes, a thriving amateur art for each to try his fortune in the cause of cultural progress. Their ideas materialized in crowd scenes, which combined theatrical action with dancing, poetry, pantomime, and recitation to music. Musicians of that school championed simple melodies of slogans, march beats and group singing. Their mouthpiece was *Pro-*

letarian Musician magazine, which proclaimed from its pages: "For a proletarian composer, the path to the song of the masses is the only correct path to follow in music." These musicians rarely and cautiously ventured beyond the music of songs and marches, declaring that serious instrumental music was not a pressing necessity for the time being.

The Association of Modern Music (AMM), formed in 1924, was an affiliation of musicians of the new school, who announced dissemination of innovative Soviet and foreign music as one of their main aims. They were particularly active in Leningrad, which was the country's artistic capital in the 1920's. Music by Stravinsky and Prokofiev, Hindemith and Krenek, Mosolov and Berg, was played in the theaters and concert halls, and many Western composers made their first visits to the Soviet Republic at the AMM's invitation. On the eve of premieres, *Modern Music* magazine regularly published articles about composers unknown to the general public and detailed commentaries on compositions to be performed. Music education of the public was another important area of work carried out by Leningrad musicologists, Boris Asafiev, Ivan Sollertinsky, Belyayev and Kushnarev among them.

The Russian Association of Proletarian Musicians (RAPM), an affiliation of followers of the other new schools, was engaged in equally energetic activities. Millions of amateur performers and members of political groups associated themselves with music in the circles of RAPM friends. The Soviet mass song of the masses and choirs flourished under the expert guidance of RAPM composers, such as Davidenko, Koval and Bely, to mention but a few.

To us, wisened by the experience of the decades which have elapsed since then, much of what was going on is clear today. To them, however, it was hardly clear in the heat of debates. For all the difference in their methods, they were very close to one another in the aims all of them pursued. Both RAPM and AMM — each in its own right — searched for what mattered most, for ways of evolving a new language of art in which to embody the new imagery of the time and a new social ideal. Indeed, in that search one could by no means afford to ignore either the enormous experience of the progressive artists of the West or the wealth of the means of expression inherent in folk music.

In retrospect, we can see and understand much. In their day, however, the passion of the polemic kept the opponents too far apart, often against their will. "He who is not with us is against us" was their motto.

Even the First All-Russia Musical Conference of 1929, called upon to pool the efforts of the leading schools, failed to bring about a reconciliation between the warring factions. In the long dispute, the voice of RAPM proved more powerful, and it finally absorbed AMM and became the main force on the musical front, seeking to subordinate to its influence music publishers, conservatories of music, concert organizations and public opinion. A similar process was in evidence, along an even harder line, within the literary community, where the omnipotent RAPP, the acronym for the Russian Association of Proletarian Writers, reigned supreme. Recalling Mayakovsky's fate, Victor Shklovsky wrote bitterly: "Mayakovsky went to RAPP only to be closer to his worker audience. He found himself in a blind alley surrounded by bans and restrictions on all sides." Eventually RAPM, which had shut itself in by a rigid framework of the hymnic intonations and rhythms of the song of the masses, doomed itself to extinction, gradually bogging down in stereotypes, hack work and dogma.

Students and new graduates of the Conservatories were living through a period of reappraisal of values. For many it was a painful and dramatic process aggravated by the restructuring of the entire system of instruction which had already been started at the Conservatories. What was since time immemorial regarded as true and immutable was now called into question and revised.

For Shostakovich the summer of 1926 was a time of anxiety and hesitation. He was plagued by the oppressive sensations of the inadequacies of the system that had raised him. The record of the past suddenly began to seem narrow like the limits of an ABC book, what he composed no longer satisfied him, and even the success of his symphony now looked doubtful.

> "For a brief time after my graduation from the Conservatory, I was haunted by doubts about my calling as a composer. I was absolutely unable to compose, and in a fit of 'disillusionment' I destroyed almost all my manuscripts. Now I regret that very much . . ."
>
> Dmitry Shostakovich, "Reflections on the Past,"
> *Soviet Music*, 1956, No. 9.

He would recall later that he began to study with all the passion of youth compositions by Stravinsky, Prokofiev, Hindemith and Krenek, at whom members of the Conservatory community simply shrugged their shoulders. His ambition to liberate himself from the canons of tradition at all costs, to venture into new ground and to assess his own self at its true worth forced him to supplement his knowledge of musical literature intensively and quickly, to augment his listening memory. The result of this liberation was the piano sonata *October*.

Critics differed in their judgments. Some delightedly heard in the sonata an escapade, a protest, a rupture with the past. Others saw in it nothing but a cut-and-dried, cumbersome and fatiguing demonstration of dexterity. Still others discerned in this work clear signs of eclecticism and formal experimentation. Steinberg was ruefully silent.

Of course, all these elements were present in Shostakovich's piano sonata to varying degrees. Shostakovich was still alive to influences, but he had already won an unchallenged right to experiment. Now that his period of disillusionment had passed, he played the sonata with confidence, unembarrassed by the discouraging reaction of the audience. In later years the assessment of the new composition was established categorically and for good; the sonata overturned the prevailing consensus. Its conflicts and drama, its hardness and dynamic motion, its romanticism and exaltation are a reflection of its time — *its* times, conflicts and drama, hardness and dynamic motion, romanticism and exaltation. This is a portrait of the country and of the composer himself in their youth.

"Dear Leonid Vladimirovich,

"In February or in March the Chopin International Piano Contest will be held in Warsaw (for entrants under 28 years of age). I wish [Vladimir] Sofronitsky and Shostakovich were among the Russian contenders. They must show themselves to the world's critics."

Excerpt from a letter by Boleslav Yavorsky to Leonid Nikolayev, December 9, 1926.

The contest, organized in connection with the unveiling of a monument to Chopin in Warsaw, was to begin on January 23, 1927. The program was made up exclusively of Chopin's compositions and looked quite modest by today's standards. In the first solo round: Polonaise in F-sharp minor, two preludes — F-sharp minor and B-flat minor — and by choice, a ballad, two études, two nocturnes, two mazurkas. In the second round: one of the two concertos for piano and orchestra.

There was very little time left. Having put off for a month composition, visits to concerts and get-togethers with friends, Shostakovich got down to work on the contest program with full concentration and clarity of purpose, as usual. He was coached by Nikolayev.

A few days before he left for Warsaw, on January 14, 1927, an audition was held in the Grand Hall of the Moscow Conservatory. It was a review of the young blood of Soviet pianism and the country's leading piano schools. Four musicians were selected: Lev Oborin (K.N. Igumnov's class), Grigory Ginzburg (A.B. Goldenweiser's class), Yuri Bryushkov (K.A. Kipp's class), all from Moscow, and Dmitry Shostakovich (L.V. Nikolayev's class) of Leningrad. They were the first envoys of the Soviet performing arts to go abroad.

"... In his manner of execution, Shostakovich of Leningrad brings us to the forefront the poetical essence of compositions; his playing is temperamental and picturesque, but his purely pianistic technique has not yet been worked up to perfection."

Music and Revolution, 1927, No. 2.

The last few days before the contest were spent on correcting technical imperfections, and on January 21 the Soviet entrants were on their way.

Warsaw met them with apprehensive silence but after the contest gave them an enthusiastic send-off. The first prize was won by Lev Oborin. "It was with heavy heart that the jury awarded the first prize to a non-Pole." (*Slowo,* Warsaw, February 1927). Ginzburg came off with the fourth prize, and Bryushkov and Shostakovich were awarded diplomas of honor.

"Dear Mother,

"Now the contest is over. I am not upset in the least, since I did my part as best I could. I played the program quite well, to my mind, and was greeted with plenty of applause. Along with eight other entrants, I was chosen to play the concerto with orchestral accompaniment. It was a great success . . . The audience welcomed me warmly and burst into an ovation the moment I finished. Everybody congratulated me as a likely candidate for the first prize, along with Oborin. The press lavished praise on the Soviet pianists as the best in the field. If anybody is to get those four prizes, they should certainly go to the Soviet contenders. That seemed to be the consensus. The jury, with a 'heavy heart,' awarded the first prize to a Russian, Lev Oborin. The choice of the other winners, however, left the public completely mystified. I was awarded a diploma of honor. When Maliszewski reading the list of awards missed my name, there were shouts from the audience: 'Shostakovich! Shostakovich!' followed by applause. Then Maliszewski read my name, and there was a stormy ovation, rather demonstrative. You needn't be worried about me. An impresario has just come over to discuss the terms of my guest tour. I shall go to Berlin next week, and on Saturday, February 5, I shall take part in a concert in Warsaw. I kiss you fondly. Give my love to Zoya and Maria. I miss all of you badly, so after a brief stay in Berlin, I will go right back home.

Yours,
Dmitry."

After the contest, the Soviet pianists gave a few solo recitals in Warsaw, Lodz, Krakow and Poznan. In addition, Oborin and Shostakovich went to Berlin for guest performances. The four young musicians, each with a striking individuality and with its own distinctive interpretation of Chopin's music, gave a splendid account of themselves as representatives of the Soviet school of pianism. Passionate temperament and sincerity, classical austerity and romantic uplift, seriousness and lyricism—that was Chopin at his best. This interpretation of the great Polish composer's music left the audiences spellbound.

On his return home, Shostakovich underwent an appendectomy. (He had felt the pains since the early days of the contest.) Quickly thereafter, at one go, in fact, he composed ten graphic piano miniatures, which were immediately christened "aphorisms" by Yavorsky and described, not so aptly, as "formalisms" by critics.

These works were based on the traditional "minor forms" honored by time and canons: the serenade, the nocturne, the march, the lullaby, etc. The very titles of these pieces seemed to indicate their mood and images. One hears in the serenade an excited and incoherent murmur to a convulsive guitar accompaniment; the nocturne cries out to three fortes; the legend turns out to be a dry and quick étude; and the lullaby frightens one by its cautious steps and mysterious rustles.

That was liberation just as in the Sonata, a liberation from canons that was openly polemic and hard, full of paradoxes and wit. The ten pieces in merry masks ridiculed the aesthetic ideal of orthodoxy and showed at the same time that the nocturne, the march and the lullaby could be heard in a new and different way.

The tenth anniversary of the October Revolution stirred a new wave of musical events. In the summer of 1927, the first musical Olympiad was held in Leningrad under the motto "Amateur Art for the Masses." The Grand Drama Theatre prepared for the jubilee a gala performance entitled "Ten Octobers," and rehearsals were in full swing for a mass heroic battle act, "The Storming of Perekop."

In the spring of that year, the music-propaganda department of the State Publishing House had asked Shostakovich to write a composition for the red-letter day. He got down to work with enthusiasm, since he had long been prepared to handle that theme. Toward the beginning of autumn, he submitted to his music publishers the score of his Second Symphony, which he had just completed—the one-movement *Dedication to October*.

The idea of his new composition was similar to that in the works of most Soviet composers in the 1920's. The theme was simple: the spreading out of gigantic forces in motion, from darkness to light, from chaos to harmony, from instinctive protest to revolutionary awareness. This idea had long taken hold of Russia's best artistic minds, from Maxim Gorky's novel *Mother,* Alexander Blok's epic poem, *The Twelve* and Vladimir Mayakovsky's *Mystery Buff* to Alexei Tolstoy's novel *Ordeal* and Mikhail Sholokhov's *And Quiet Flows the Don.* However, whereas poetry and prose had been able to go far from naive illustration and verbose rhetoric, music on the theme of Revolution was still in its infancy. In fact, Soviets were teaching the art of music to others and learning (still learning!) this art themselves. The ABC's of music are harder to learn than the alphabet.

Shostakovich's symphony was one of many such experiments. His experiment, however, was unusually talented, bold and vivid. Small wonder, therefore, that he became the winner of the first prize for the best October Revolution anniversary composition.

For all his knowledge and deep appreciation of belles-lettres, he chose for the choral finale A. Bezymensky's declarative and symbolic verses, which Bezymensky himself would later *not* list among his creative achievements. But let us be lenient; at the time his verses seemed the best and most effective choice for Shostakovich.

The means of expression he had chosen were distinguished by a maximum of simplicity and vividness. Darkness and chaos were conveyed by the rigidity of harmonies and the powerful roar of basses; struggle and uplift by dynamic motion downward and upward; the radiance of victory by the hyperbolic resonance of the colossal chorus. Was it naive? Perhaps. Was it much too illustrative? It certainly was. Nevertheless, this music is incredibly expressive and forceful. How symbolic, indeed, is the factory whistle opening the finale! Not perfect, not mature in every detail, this nonetheless is a worthy monument of its time.

The music of the symphony—its grotesquely hard language with its screeching and hooting sounds and noise—is inspired with faith and sincerity, which adds much to its power. Shostakovich was keenly responsive to the ideals and accomplishments of his stormy time, and his *Dedication to October*, like his *October* sonata, proclaimed the civic-mindedness he had displayed even as a nine-year-old boy in his piano pieces "Soldier," "A Hymn to Freedom," and "A Funeral March in Memory of Revolutionary Martyrs."

"That concert was Moscow's first review of symphonic works on the revolutionary theme. . . . Shostakovich's symphonic *Dedication to October* proved to be the most colorful and significant of all compositions on the repertoire. Performed by a choir and orchestra, this work, with its enormous emotional appeal and maximum exertion of the will, is the embodiment of life, movement and struggle in music. The majestic and colorful sounds of the concluding chorus enthralled the audience. A tremendous force of impression emanates from the final declamatory bursts of the chorus "October-Commune-Lenin" and is reinforced by the dry sforzato of the small drum—just like the decisive blow struck by the Revolution. . . . It must be acknowledged that the revolutionary theme did not force the young composer to change or simplify his identity even slightly, but, on the contrary, encouraged him to reveal in comprehensive detail his thriving creativity in this composition."

Music and Revolution, 1927, No. 12.

The premiere of *Dedication to October* was held on the very eve of the holiday—on November 6, 1927—in Leningrad. It was welcomed by both the AMM and RAPM with equal delight, since it expressed the aspirations of both. How bored, indeed, one would feel to hear the cliché words "leftism" and "formalism" with which this unusual composition would be labelled later.

A Farce

"See here," a stern-faced comrade once addressed us. "Why do you write what is amusing? Why chuckle in a reconstruction period? Are you out of your mind?" Then he lectured us angrily and at length about the harm caused by humor now. "It's not a laughing matter. To laugh is blasphemy," he said. "Even to smile is too much. When I see this new life, this great change around us, I don't feel like laughing. I feel an urge to pray."

"But we don't simply crack jokes," we protested. "We satirize those who are blind to the reconstruction period."

"Satire cannot be funny," the stern-faced comrade declared.
(Ilya Ilf and Evgeny Petrov, *The Little Golden Calf,* 1931.)

They did not laugh at their time; they admired it. They mocked individuals unworthy of that great time: those who held onto the petty attributes of comfortable living in their homes and were absolutely indifferent to the changing life around them. True, those "respectable" petty bourgeois were on their way to extinction in the new society. They agonized but not as quickly as one would desire. As their existence grew more and more senseless, their mentality became increasingly licentious and aggressive. That was the mad, meaningless gallop of agony. The petty bourgeoisie had already caused grave harm and was trying to cause more. That is why the artists with their keen power of observation examined the ugly world of the philistines and recoiled in disgust. Without a moment's hesitation, they undertook the difficult task of fighting whatever is mean and insulting to human dignity. They were guided by their awareness of their commitment as artists who had always fought against evil whatever mask it might wear. Whether it was dressed in the mink coats of the nouveau riche, the flashy vests of foppish snobs, or the brown shirts of storm troopers, evil in any situation tended toward proliferation, total conformity and total domination. They realized that with crystal clarity. For them, evil was personified, in particular, by the petty bourgeoisie, still alive, still poisoning the air and hence extremely dangerous. It was necessary to fight these greedy members of society immediately, on the spot. Therefore, art levelled against them its most formidable and lethal weapon, satire.

They were not afraid to come down from the sterling integrity of a refined literary style to the banal and vulgar language of their "heroes" of the petty bourgeois stamp, who should more properly be called "anti-heroes." They knew that someone had to take care of this subject, after all. In their works the primitive protozoan existence of the petty bourgeois was magnified, as if under a microscope, exposing the stupidity and frightening senselessness of his life. They wrote novels and short stories, verses and poems, plays and topical satire. They made drawings and staged plays, cracked jokes and played pranks with an imperturbable look, and they jointly sculptured a large, grotesque mask of the petty bourgeoisie.

They united under the flag of the Blue Blouse Society, the Russian News Agency's display windows, and simply on the basis of complete mutual understanding. Among them were Vladimir Mayakovsky, Mikhail Zoshchenko, Daniel Harms, Nikolai Oleinikov, Ilya Ilf, Evengy Petrov, Nikolai Radlov, Evgeny Schwartz, Sergei Radlov, Vsevolod Meyerhold, Mikhail Bulgakov and Nikolai Zabolotsky.

And, of course, Dmitry Shostakovich. He was perhaps the first of the composers of his time to have resolutely stepped over the abyss between "high" and "low" art. The latter—profuse commercial products that flooded the market—constituted the kind of workday music that AMM and RAPM and the academics were too squeamish to deal with. Thieves' jargon lyrics, the philistine romance, the vulgarity of cancan and fox-trot, the banality of the operetta—Shostakovich was not interested in these genres as such, but he turned them to advantage as a means of parodic denunciation, unafraid of losing his balance and slipping into the quagmire of vulgarism.

While working on *Dedication to October*, Shostakovich was collecting material for his opera *The Nose*. But what about consistency, one might wonder. Revolutionary passion on the one hand and satire on the other? Bezymensky's rhetorical verse and the grotesque of Gogol's prose? The most up-to-date subject and a farce of the times of Tzar Nicholas I? It seemed an unthinkable mixture. Such mixtures, however unexpected and bizarre, constituted the fabric of the time, and as an artist, observant and quick on the uptake, he was responsive to all phenomena of life.

Besides, he had reached the age of adulthood—21 years. (At that age, his grandfather had gone through the gruelling trials of exile). The forceful seriousness of the Second Symphony did not make him blind to the mindless world of the petty bourgeoisie. He sensed his duty as a musician to denounce this world angrily, sharply, intransigently, and he boldly took up a theme nobody before him had dared to work out on such a broad scale in Soviet music. By the satirical message of *The Nose*, the composer asserted his civic position just as firmly as he had asserted it by the romantic and lofty message of the symphony *Dedication to October*.

"The fairy story about Major Kovalev, who lost his nose, has been turned into a deadly satire of human meanness ... The music has destroyed the narrow historical framework of the characters, summed them up and shown them as living beings, even as our contemporaries."

I. Sollertinsky, *The Nose* Shostakovich, 1930.

The problem of Soviet opera had long been in the air. The cumbersome genre sanctified by tradition and the predilections of music lovers was lending itself to renovation with difficulty. The Central Repertoire Committee set up in 1923 strove to influence the repertoire by every means at its disposal, but implicit faith in the magic power of decrees produced no comforting results.

Attempts were undertaken to remake old operas along new lines. Mikhail Glinka's *A Life for the Tsar*, for instance, was transformed, without changing the music, into the opera *Hammer and Sickle*, and Giacomo Meyerbeer's *The Huguenots* into *The Decembrists*. New operas on revolutionary and historical subjects were composed, but the new content could not be forced into the procrustean bed of the customary roles and plots of the classical forms. A few operas of that period—*For Red Petrograd* by Gladkovsky and Prussak, *The Eagles' Revolt* by Pashchenko, and *Stepan Razin* by Triodin—have survived to date only in textbooks and encyclopedias as distinctive artifacts of their time. Russia's theatrical and musical life, flowing over the setbacks and regrets of experiments, continued its course in the majestic mainstream of a few classical operas joined by a motley stream of operettas. There were occasional foreign "visitors"—*Nightingale* by Igor Stravinsky, *Salome* by Richard Strauss, *Wozzeck* by Alban Berg.

The need for radical reforms in opera was felt by all, but attempts to find new approaches in this medium invariably failed. The turning of the tide came with Shostakovich's opera *The Nose*, which musicologist Ivan Sollertinsky would later describe as "the first original opera written in Soviet territory by a Soviet composer."

For Shostakovich the idea of an opera on Nikolai Gogol's short story "The Nose" was not a sudden stroke of genius. He had long searched for a subject in modern literature and then turned to the classics: Saltykov-Shchedrin, Chekhov and Gogol. Finally he chose "The Nose."

There was a new revival of interest in Gogol in those years. The tragicomical beginning of his works, the lapses from the prosaic into the phantasmagoric, burlesque and lofty romanticism—all these were consonant with the times. In 1926, Yuri Tynyanov produced a screen version of *The Overcoat*, and Vsevolod Meyerhold and Igor Terentyev, each in his own city, staged plays based on *The Inspector-General*.

"There was much talk about me [Gogol] and some of my qualities, but my main essence escaped attention. It was visible to Pushkin alone. He told me more than once that no writer had yet possessed this talent to expose so vividly the banality of life, to portray so forcefully the triviali-

A scene from the 1974 production of *The Nose* at the Moscow Chamber Theatre.

Opposite:
Shostakovich with one of his best friends, the outstanding music critic Ivan Sollertinsky. Leningrad, the 1930s.

ty of the trivial man and make all the details eluding the eye strikingly apparent to all."

Nikolai Gogol, *Selected Excerpts From Correspondence with Friends,* 1843.

In March 1927, Shostakovich saw in the Press House *The Inspector-General* directed by Terentyev, and in September he saw this comedy staged by Meyerhold's visiting company. In the autumn he completed the preparation of the libretto of *The Nose* and went over his numerous sketches of the music. Some of his drafts were mingled with themes from *Dedication to October.*

One day in early January 1928, when he was hard at work on the opera in his apartment on Marat Street, there was an unexpected telephone call. Meyerhold was speaking. "I want to see you. Come on over, if you can. I'll be waiting for you in my hotel room." Shostakovich complied, and in a few days he was enrolled on the staff of the Meyerhold Theater in Moscow (GOSTIM) as music director and pianist. He had agreed to this job without a moment's hesitation and was soon on his way to the capital, carrying sketches of his opera in his luggage.

Shostakovich had seen a few of Meyerhold's productions: *Masquerade,* based on Mikhail Lermontov's novel; *The Forest,* after Nikolai Ostrovsky's; *Trust D.E.,* after Ilya Ehrenburg's; *The Mandate,* after Erdmann's. He knew a good deal about Meyerhold from his Conservatory student colleague Leo Arnstam, who was now a pianist at GOSTIM. He remembered Meyerhold as he had seen him at the performance of *The Inspector-General* in Leningrad: a defiant figure with an arm thrust forward, a shock of hair, the beak-like nose of a predator—a fighting-cock of a man fiercely bowing to that part of the audience who were booing him vehemently. Public interest in this art director was enormous.

Shostakovich's duties at the theater were simple. He played the piano—now in the orchestra, now on the stage—and occasionally compilations of musical passages for rehearsals and performances. The rest of the time—there were long intervals between productions—passed in discussion, conversation and reflection. For the first time he found himself in a circle of like-minded comrades engaged in collective, creative work. Igor Ilyinsky, Erast Garin, Zinaida Reich, Lev Sverdlin, Sergei Martinson and Vasily Zaichikov—GOSTIM's finest actors—worked enthusiastically under the master's inspired schemes. There was no inertness or calm in the theater, and there were no quiet premieres. Shostakovich lived in Meyerhold's apartment, played much and engaged in heated debates with his host.

"... There was much fascinating for me at that theater. And the most wonderful of all were rehearsals under Meyerhold's direction. His work on his new productions was unusually captivating, literally enthralling ... I admired *The Inspector-General* most of all, perhaps because it had something in common with my work on *The Nose.*

Dmitry Shostakovich, "The Year 1928 . . .," *Theater*, 1974, No. 2.

Indeed, *The Inspector-General* and *The Nose* have much in common in their choice of subject, in their social message, in the grotesque character of their productions, in the structure and principles of organization of action and in other elements. Shostakovich borrowed much from Meyerhold's art direction. He himself admitted that he "had begun to compose music in a somewhat different manner." Perhaps it was thanks to this influence that he sculptured the gigantic eccentric mask of *The Nose*, his first composition for the stage with such classical maturity and precision.

However, let us not reduce all the merits of the opera to imitation of the master by the pupil. They were both working for a common cause, each a little in his own way. Piotrovsky was tirelessly experimenting on the theatrical stage and in the films. Lopukhov and Leonid Jacobson were restructuring Soviet ballet, Sokolovsky was setting up the Working Youth Theater (TRAM). Sergei Eisenstein, Grigory Kozintsev and Trauberg were doing their innovative work at the Sovkino film studios on Yasniye Zori Street in Leningrad. Each of them was a jack-of-all-trades, combining the talents of art director, decor designer, cameraman, ballet master, and dancer. Their productions were equally universal, with elements of theatrical art, cinematography, poster display and circus performance. This was called the art of the '20s, and *The Nose* was a legitimate child of its time.

At first glance, the composer preserved in *The Nose* everything that any decent opera was supposed to have: an orchestral introduction, arias, ensembles, and magnificent finales. But what grimace of mockery distorted their respectable appearance! Convulsive patter instead of a cantilena; a quartet in which the partners neither hear nor see one another because they are in different houses of St. Petersburg; an ensemble of eight yard keepers without the slightest sign of harmony or euphony; and so on and so forth. In the whirlwind movement of scenes, cancans, galops and polkas follow in rapid succession, the orchestra chirps, amazing the listener with its unimaginable timbres, the chorus of idlers puffs, excited by the goings-on, and the percussion instruments nervously keep time in pursuit of the Nose. The music unfolds, in continuous action, "an improbable accident" with Major Kovalev's nose, in which are involved yard keepers and cross-buns, policemen and umbrellas, a barber and a Persian prince.

At the composer's will, the opera form is divorced at all structural levels from the habitual content, just as the most habitual things and concepts are divorced by the rules of this paradoxical game from their intrinsic forms of being. Major Kovalev receives from Podtochina an answer to his letter, which has not yet been read by Podtochina herself; the crowd, en masse, energetically pursues the Nose, while . . . standing still. Time is turned backward, movement turns out to be immobility—everything is caricatured, down to the immutable laws of nature.

Actor Edouard Akimov as Major Kovalev in *The Nose*, at the Moscow Chamber Music Theatre.

Nikolai Gogol, on whose satirical short story *The Nose* Shostakovich based his opera.

Shostakovich and conductor Gennady Rozhdestvensky at a rehearsal of *The Nose* at the Chamber Music Theatre, in June 1973.

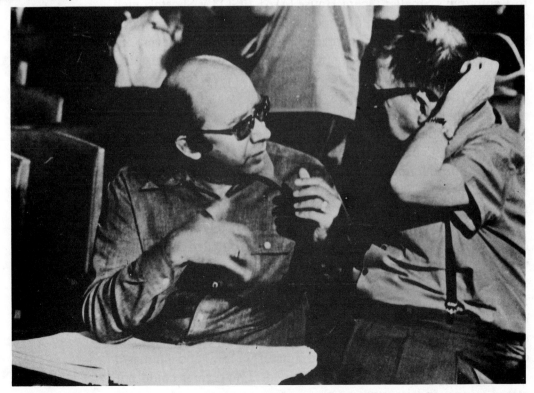

This technique was not (as, say, in the *Aphorisms*) simply a brilliant discovery by an innovative artist accustomed to calling in question all canons (although this motive was present in the art of his comrades of the satirical genre). Nor was this technique just an attack by an innovative artist against a decrepit genre covered by a spiderweb of traditions. It had been suggested to Shostakovich by the entire romantic style and structure of Gogol's story, which turned inside out the whole life of the Imperial Russia of Nicholas I, where the Nose existed separately from Major Kovalev just as the human personality itself was estranged from reality.

It would be naive to seek elementary current analogies in the opera and to regard it only as a satirical portrait of the petty bourgeoisie of the 1920s, as has been done by many of Shostakovich's contemporaries. True, it certainly contains this element, too, because Gogol's immortal fantasy is all-pervasive. But the story and the opera based on it are infinitely richer than any interpretation linking their universal satire directly to some time in the past or present.

Shostakovich completed the opera in Leningrad after quitting his job at GOSTIM and returning home.

> ". . . In the same year I left the theater for good. There was too much technical work there. I had not found work for myself that would have satisfied me and Meyerhold at the same time . . ."
>
> Dmitry Shostakovich, "In the Year 1928 . . ." *Theater,* 1974, No. 2.

In the autumn of 1929, the opera was completed and submitted to Leningrad's Smaller Opera House (MALEGOT). Shostakovich sent a copy of the score to Moscow. He wanted *The Nose* to be staged by Meyerhold. The pressure of business, however, interfered with the latter's plans to produce the opera, so its first night in Moscow took place decades later—in 1974.

Among Leningrad's theaters MALEGOT was known as the most ardent supporter of experiments and quests for innovative ideas. Its Artistic-Political Council announced that the theater was "entering on the path of resolute Sovietization of the opera repertoire," and production of *The Nose* was enthusiastically taken up by chief art director Samuel Samosud, art director Nikolai Smolich, and decor designer Vladimir Dmitriyev.

The company liked the opera almost immediately. The singers, one of whom was to sing his part with his nose pinched throughout the action, quickly appreciated the convenience and naturalness of the vocal parts, which were by no means simple or melodious. Rehearsals were conducted with inspiration and keen attention to detail. All were aware of the singular significance of the new production. They were to present to the audience the first Soviet opera, which was novel in subject, dramaturgy, form and language.

The premiere, however, was postponed. The theater could not afford to suspend its work on the current repertoire. Many new productions were to be staged in the 1928-29 season, and, besides, assimilation of the unusual material of *The Nose* required considerable time.

In March 1928, the premiere was finally announced in Leningrad, and on June 16 a concert performance of *The Nose* was held for representatives of various artistic organizations. Opinions differed, but the date of the premiere was fixed unanimously: January 18, 1930.

"The scenery designed by Vladimir Dmitriyev was turning and whirling to the accompaniment of rollicking galops and dashing polkas; Gogol's phantasmagoria was translated into sound and color. The distinctive imagery of young Russian art associated with daring experimentation in the field of form and with urban folklore—the signboards of shops and pubs, bands at cheap dancehalls—burst its way into the realm of *Aida* and *Il Trovatore*. Gogol's grotesque was in its element: what was a farce and what was a prophesy here?

"Fantastic orchestral combinations, texts that were unthinkable to sing, unusual rhythms . . . assimilation of all that had formerly seemed unpoetical, unmusical and vulgar but was, in fact, a living intonation, a parody—a fight against convention. . . .

"It was a very funny spectacle."
Grigory Kozintsev, *The Space of Tragedy*, 1973.

The first reaction of critics—consternation—was surprisingly similar to the final scene in *The Inspector-General*. But it did not last long. "Satire cannot be funny," the stern-faced comrades said and marched ahead in serried ranks.

"One cannot regard all this as a Soviet opera . . . Only a few formal elements can be used subsequently for the construction of a truly proletarian opera . . . and that, of course, on a different theme and in pursuance of a different purpose."
Krasnaya Gazeta (The Red Gazette) evening issue, January 20, 1930.

"To speak of *The Nose* as a Soviet opera the mass of the listeners are waiting for would be wrong, of course."
Krasnaya Gazeta, morning issue, January 24, 1930.

"The subject of *The Nose* is in no way related to the themes of interest to the modern spectator."
The Worker and the Theater, 1930, No. 7.

"Shostakovich was without question attracted by the sexual undertones . . . *The Nose* is a great experiment standing aloof from the mainstream of Soviet opera and discrepant with the composer's own self."
The Workers and the Theater, 1930, No. 5.

There was another, different comment, it is true. "What dark glasses one must have hooked onto one's nose to discern in the opera subject anything like mysticism or sex! . . . But let us turn to the music. Here are a few facts. Do they really stand apart from the mainstream of Soviet opera?

"Shostakovich has done away with the traditional forms of opera and made it impossible for this art to relapse into anything like *Stepan Razin* or *Ivan the Soldier*.

"He has shown opera composers the need to evolve a new musical language, discarding the threadbare cliches of imitators of Tchaikovsky or Rimsky-Korsakov.

"He has produced a fascinating experiment in music based on rhythm and timbre alone.

"With his perky, biting rhythms, he has lent dynamic motion to the normally slow opera scenes, thereby bringing opera close to the techniques of the modern theater.

"He may be the first composer in Russian opera to have made his heroes talk in living language rather than pour themselves out in stilted arias and cantilenas.

"Thanks to Shostakovich, composers will no longer make the listeners blush for shame at hearing iron-willed commissars singing sugary ariosos à la Lensky. . .

"Does this music, nevertheless, really lie outside the plan of reconstructing Soviet opera?"

The Workers and the Theater, 1930, No. 7.

But this puzzling question of Sollertinsky's in his brilliant article *"The Nose:* A Long-Range Gun," just like Meyerhold's unconditional "Good!" was ignored by many. A heated debate flared up between supporters of the opera, who were heavily outnumbered, and its opponents, and the controversy lasted through a few issues of *The Worker and the Theater*. The antagonists argued not so much about the opera itself as about the development of Soviet opera in general, about its methods, tasks and opportunities.

The Nose was run 16 times: 14 in the 1929-30 season and twice in the 1930-31 season, and then vanished from the scene for a long time. The path of resolute Sovietization of the opera repertoire proved a very thorny one. In 1934 Boris Asafiev wrote a bitter afterword to a history of Shostakovich's first opera:

"The fate of *The Nose*, which is a talented opera, is very saddening. When a young composer ventured to convey through the medium of music the real message of Gogol's story and thus to deal with the 'images of the past' which troubled his imagination, he was simply accused of formalism without making any careful analysis of his art. Evidently, if Shostakovich had recounted this novella of Gogol's in the idyllically naive musical language of Rimsky-Korsakov's *May Night*, he would not have been labelled a formalist.

". . . This opera was one of the amazing events attending the emergence of a new content in the interpretation of a sinister period of St. Petersburg life and, accordingly, the emergence of a new style and new fabric of Russian opera."

Boris Asafiev, *The Art of Shostakovich and His Opera Lady Macbeth of Mtsensk*, 1934.

Shostakovich, however, was reluctant to part with the "images of the past which troubled his imagination." While preparations were under way for the production of *The Nose*, he wrote music for Vladimir Mayakovsky's play *The Bedbug*, and in the spring of 1930 he considered the idea of composing an opera to be called *The Carp*, after a short verse by N. Oleinikov. This subject held out brilliant opportunities: an underwater society, lady carps, a charming mistress, piscine passions, and what not. Unfortunately, this idea did not materialize, just like his later conceptions of an operetta after Ilf and Petrov's *The Twelve Chairs*, an opera based on Gogol's comedy *The Gamblers*, and operas taken from themes by Saltykov-Shchedrin and Chekhov.

Motion Pictures, Ballet, Theater

As soon as he completed the score of *The Nose* and submitted it to the theater, Shostakovich plunged into a weltering whirlwind of work. He wrote simultaneously music for films and dramas, a symphony and ballets, and even music-hall turns. At the same time, he engaged in intensive work as a performing musician, touring various Soviet cities with solo recitals and appearing with orchestral accompaniment. Tchaikovsky's First Piano Concerto was the leading item of his repertoire, and he played in concert with the pianist M. Yudina, the soloist L. Vyrlan and the cellist V. Kubatsky. He was not indiscriminate, but as a man of universal interests he wanted to learn and sample as much as he could.

In December 1928 he came back to the cinema. The era of motion-picture scores had just begun. Intended so far only for cinema orchestras, it was conceived as a broad musical canvas moving in counterpoint to external, silent action and revealing the psychology of the characters, placing dramaturgical accents in the film. The time of stereotypes and naive illustrations was receding into the past. The young directors Kozintsev and Trauberg chose Shostakovich to blaze the trail, requesting him to write the score for the film *The New Babylon*.

This was a romantic love story of a vendor, Louise, and a soldier, Jean, who found themselves in opposite camps at the time of the Paris Commune in the 1870s. The music for the film linked them together and explained the past and predicted the future, unraveling what was hidden and denying what was apparent. It was still a musical mosaic and thundered the "Marseillaise" with slogan-like straightforwardness in the scenes of the trimmed parks of Versailles, but it nevertheless strove to achieve complete unity, in which the love story of Louise and Jean would be a backdrop for the scenes of class battles.

The destiny of the first film score was tragicomical. Cinema orchestras flatly refused to play the new music, largely incomprehensible to them, and accused the authors of ignoring the specific requirements of the cinema. For their part, the authors rushed from one cinema to another, persuading, imploring and pressuring the orchestras to play from their score, and finally wrested consent, though it was to hold for only two or three days.

"The books of complaints in many cinemas were found to contain an indignant entry probably made by one and the same person while the film was on. It read: 'The orchestra conductor must have been drunk today!' . . . The composer was called a cheeky country bumpkin ignorant of the rules of orchestration. The score was angrily criticized. It was much simpler, of course, to live in the old way. After a few days, the irritating sounds died down. The orchestras were cheerfully playing a hot tune called 'East River Boating.' "

Grigory Kozintsev, *The Deep Screen*, 1971.

The tradition of film-music albums proved too tenacious. The film studios of Krasniye Zori Street, however, were not places where dogma would survive for long. Here they experimented with sound, testing sound quality and coming up with innovative ideas in the audio field. They built enormous structures of unusual design and crammed them with thundering sound equipment. Cinematography was learning to talk.

The next production directed by Kozintsev and Trauberg was *Alone*, a film about the fate of a schoolteacher fighting for a new life in a far-away village in the Altai Mountains. Leo Arnstam was invited to take part as sound producer and Shostakovich as composer. He wrote his second score with much greater confidence, integrating all the key dramaturgical lines of the film in symphonic development, where the main theme was "Happy Days Are Coming," the first song in Soviet cinematography. Film-music albums could no longer stem the tide of this new trend.

The Golden Mountains, a full-length sound film, was Shostakovich's third work in the cinema. As evidenced by Arnstam, the filming team included some "quite inexperienced young men": the art director, Sergei Yutkevich; the cameraman, Georges Martov; the sound producer, Leo Arnstam; and the composer, Dmitry Shostakovich. The filmmakers were to show the progress of the illiterate and downtrodden peasant Peter toward an awareness of the justice and necessity of working-class struggle. The very same idea of progress from an instinctive protest to revolutionary awareness was the keynote of the film *Alone*, just as of the Second Symphony written four years earlier.

But now Shostakovich was not a beginner but a master, thoroughly familiar with the rules of cinematography, the associations of sound with the specific qualities of motion-picture space and time. The song "If I Had Mountains of Gold" was built up into a score of truly symphonic dimensions and integrity. The future of film music was now assured. As Leo Arnstam wrote:

"Music linked by intricate ties with the spoken word and with the arrangement pattern, music lending dramaturgical unity to the film—that was the kind of music we dreamt of. Such music by definition could not be fractional, broken up into small fragments.

"Shostakovich resolved that problem in large, symphonic forms. And simple forms—for instance, the waltz. Played once by an amusement park brass band in segments on the piano during the course of the action, this waltz was developed into a large, many-faceted piece for a symphony orchestra. This piece was intimately linked with the complex scenes of the moral corruption of the main hero of the film, the very same peasant, Peter. Shostakovich boldly introduced the most complex musical forms into cinematography. His most significant achievement of principle was perhaps his fugue for the organ and a large symphony orchestra.

"Two episodes in the film—the strike in Baku and the strike in St. Petersburg—develop in parallel. There is a wide diversity of fragments in the arrangement—about 60 in all. Slow-motion scenes flash back to lightning-fast scenes of the shooting of workers demonstrating in Baku and St. Petersburg.

"That was a refined parallel arrangement, and its excellence was augmented by the rare integrity of Shostakovich's fugue. This merger proved unusually forceful and impressive in its artistic appeal."

Leo Arnstam, *Music of the Heroic,* 1977.

A year later, the "Song About the First Comer," from Shostakovich's music for the film *The First Comer,* swept the country and immediately won the hearts of all. In the years of the Second World War, its melody would become the anthem of cooperation of the United Nations. Twenty years later, Shostakovich would call *The Golden Mountains* and *The First Comer* the turning-points of his work in cinematography, during which he would compose music for another 30 films.

In the spring of 1928, when the authors of *The New Babylon* were looking for like-minded comrades in the cinema orchestras, a discussion was in progress in Soviet ballet, just as in opera, on the pressing problems involved in renewing the repertoire. One of the most inert genres of art, academic ballet assumed quite fantastic and monstrous forms under the pressure of the character dance and pantomime, but it was still holding its ground. Leningrad's opera and ballet theater (GATOB) announced a contest for the best scenario of a modern ballet, specifically indicating that this should be a review performance with a large number of mass scenes. First prize was awarded to the director Alexander Ivanovsky for his libretto of *Dynamiada.* Shostakovich was requested to write the music for the ballet. It was produced by the choreographers Vladimir Chesnakov, Vasily Vainonen and Leonid Jacobson, with Alexander Gauk as conductor and Valentina Khodasevich as set designer. The ballet was entitled *The Golden Age.*

The libretto was based on an unsophisticated story of a team of Soviet athletes visiting a Western country to attend the "Golden Age" international fair, where they had encounters with fascists. After a series of adventures, the Soviet team won all events and in conclusion performed a dance of solidarity and friendship with the Western workers. This subject offered the cast unlimited opportunities, so the ballet absorbed everything Soviet ballet art sought and aspired to in its search for a solution to the general problems facing the art of the '20s.

First, the ballet was frankly populistic. The antithesis "we" and "they" was embodied in the spirit of a gigantic symbolic political poster in which the colors were strikingly contrastive. This was manifest in Khodasevich's designs of costumes as well: the dark hues and elusive outlines of the dress of the characters of the capitalist West and the bright red-blue-yellow costumes of the Soviet team. It was also evident in Shostakovich's music: the sensual, lazy jazz tunes, the grotesque rhythms of a fox-trot and the resilient beats of a march. The central conflict of the revolutionary era—the conflict between two intransigent camps—was expressed in *The Golden Age* with declarative single-mindedness. The authors' narrowminded aesthetic position, however, was inevitable, like an infantile disorder one must outgrow.

Second, the ballet was distinctively athletic. In the world of the builders of a new life, everybody was supposed to engage in athletic pursuits. Energy, muscular strength, trimness and rhythmic movements—such were the ideal qualities of the person of the future, as they were visualized at that time. That was the guiding idea for the way in which the choreographers directed the dances of the Soviet team and for Shostakovich's choosing a march and a major key to be the main elements of his music. Significantly, the very subject of the ballet was directly associated with sports, so one may wonder if it was not for this athletic theme that Ivanovsky was awarded top prize.

Third, the ballet was a synthesis of different genres of art, like many other theatrical productions of that time. *The Golden Age* included elements of a motion picture and a circus performance, a music-hall show, a political review and a dance suite, unfolding in a series of independent or relatively unconnected episodes with a large number of mass scenes. Shostakovich's score was made up of separate musical items subordinated to the general theme, although he frankly strove for the ideal cinematographic music—integration of all elements in a large symphonic canvas.

The première of *The Golden Age* was held on October 26, 1930, and created an uproar. Lovers of classical ballet were loath to accept the athletic character of the dances, as well as Shostakovich's harsh musical language, and the critics denounced the ballet in no uncertain terms.

"One can find here frank opportunism and vulgarization of an important theme, as well as inordinate gravitation to formalism . . . How could it happen that the ideology of the bourgeois music hall, hostile to Soviet theatrical art, should have infiltrated a state ballet theater and in such an immoderate dose, for that matter?"
The Worker and the Theater, 1930, Nos. 60-61.

Before long the ballet was dropped from the repertoire, and Shostakovich, at GATOB's request again, almost immediately started to write the music for the ballet *The Bolt*, which was a natural continuation of *The Golden Age*, although another production team worked upon it: the librettist Vladimir Smirnov, the choreographer Fedor Lopukhov, the set designers Tatiana Bruni and Georgy Korshikov. In the performance, the antithesis "we" and "they" was just as straightforward, the only difference being its more local character. The scene was a factory where energetic Komsomol workers exposed time-servers and destroyers. The positive characters dreamed of a future of steel and glass. This dream materialized in the skeletal structures of constructivist stage scenery, in workers' dances imitating the operation of pistons, engines and flywheels, and in the solemn and majestic march rhythms of Shostakovich's music. That was the music of shock troops and Red Army men.

The negative characters were concentrated in the second, central act. Here Shostakovich was in his element. The satirical pungency of the music of *The Bolt* was in places even more impressive than certain scenes in *The Nose*. Hysterical young women, bureaucrats, botchers, philistines passed in a long and vivid series, and at the end of the act they plunged into a disgusting orgy to the blaring accompaniment of tawdry commercial music.

Just as in *The Golden Age*, Shostakovich failed in his effort to produce an integral symphonic canvas in this ballet. The reason was not a lack of determination but active resistance on the part of the very nature of the process of critical review.

The première of *The Bolt*, held on April 8, 1931, was a total failure. The criticism was devastating, although the ballet fully complied with the directive issued by GATOB regarding its ballet-scenario contest to produce a modern review.

In the autumn of 1929, without interrupting his other work, Shostakovich wrote his Third Symphony, *May Day*. Just like the Second Symphony, it consisted of only one movement with a concluding chorus to a text by S. Kirsanov, but it was much unlike the Second's allegorical, abstract theme and dry and hard language, although chronologically there was a space of only two years between the two symphonies.

His work in the theater and in film had produced its effect. The new symphony was powerful in its imagery, closely resembling in form the fleeting scenes of various events in a newsreel. . . . Now a bugle sang and a column of Young Pioneers marched off along the street; now it was a green forest landscape in May and the anxious atmosphere of a clandestine May Day meeting; and now cavalrymen galloped across the screen, their swinging, shining sabres almost touching the spectators.

The symphony was filled with music about the first Five-Year Plan—music of the youth groups Young Pioneers and the Komsomols—the heroic sounds of trumpets, with a rich gamut of melodies. The inspiration of peaceful construction lent it a festive quality and freshness, while the concluding chorus sounded solemnly and majestically (although Kirsanov's verses differed but little from those of Bezymensky). The symphony resembled most of all a one-movement poetic elegy of the hero of its time with the spontaneity and sincerity of youth.

One day early in 1929, Shostakovich received a telephone call from Meyerhold. The eminent director again offered him work at GOSTIM—but now not as a pianist and music director but as a composer. He was to write the music for Mayakovsky's play *The Bedbug*. Shostakovich accepted without hesitation. He was attracted by the prospect of working with Meyerhold, the atmosphere of creativity in the theater, and the opportunity for close association with Mayakvosky.

Shostakovich composed more than 20 pieces for *The Bedbug*. Some of them fascinated him with their novelty, since they were intended for unfamiliar instruments: the button-key accordion and the brass band. He wrote the pieces for GOSTIM's brilliant accordion trio with obvious pleasure, and the galop for the accordion timbre sounded especially boisterous. The idea of including a brass band in his score crossed his mind after his first meeting with Mayakovsky. The poet's first question was, "Do you like firemen's brass bands?" He realized after some time that it was precisely the music of brass bands (trumpets, French horns and trombones), shrill and vulgar, that would worthily crown the finale of the first act and lend it a satirical quality.

The production of *The Bedbug* was prepared by Meyerhold jointly with Mayakovsky, the Kukryniks trio of cartoonists, and the artist Alexander Rodchenko, while Igor Ilyinsky rehearsed the part of Prisypkin. Opening night was a great success. Shostakovich's music emphasized the dramatic highlights in the play, imparting a militant satirical tone. The critics later specifically pointed out the complete harmony between the musical score and dramaturgy of *The Bedbug*.

> "Soviet opera will be born of the music of modern drama
> rather than creep out of old opera art by an evolutionary
> route. Soviet opera is inconceivable outside modern
> theatrical culture."
> *Zhizn Iskusstva (The Life of Art),* 1929, No. 18.

In the disputes over the problems of Soviet opera and the wider problems of Soviet music in general, one could hear increasingly insistent appeals for learning from the dramatic theater, which had found new themes, new imagery and new means of expression earlier than any other genre of art after the October Revolution. The loudest calls were coming from Boris Asafiev and Ivan Sollertinsky, musicians with whom Shostakovich was associated especially closely. It was under their influence that he joined the company of TRAM.

The Working Youth Theater set up by Mikhail Sokolovsky had been conceived as an amateur company of Komsomols and young production workers. In Sokolovsky's view, the theater was called upon to propagandize exclusively modern plays dealing with the problems of young people's daily lives and work and with the struggle against religious and bourgeois prejudices, and thus to assist young people's education and enlightenment. TRAM's productions were openly populist, serving political-agitation purposes, and their style invariably inspired its following.

Shostakovich entered the TRAM company with an intention to see at close range the young workers' lives, interests and impassioned quests for new approaches in theatrical art. He wrote music for three plays: Bezymensky's *The Shot*, about the struggle of young workers in a railroad yard against bureaucrats (almost a replica of *The Bolt*); Gorbenko and Lvov's *Virgin Lands,* about socialist collectivization in the countryside; and Piotrovsky's *Rule, Britannia!* about the life of workers abroad.

Attracted by the spirit of TRAM's plays, Shostakovich composed music for them—marches, songs and satirical pieces—with pleasure and ease. Very soon, however, he approached the point beyond which he would be doomed to mechanical work, turning out stereotyped incidental music in the manner of the notorious film-music albums. The predetermined events in the plot predetermined the mode of thinking of the composer and probably of the art director, and inertia in their approach to problems entailed inertia in the resolution of these problems. This threatened the dramatic theater as well as opera and ballet. In the spring of 1931, when Shostakovich started composing the music for *Rule, Britannia!* he already sensed this danger from his previous work on *The Bedbug, The Golden Age* and *The Bolt.*

The stilted and placardlike character of incidental music bored him more and more, and the pile of orders from the theater was growing on his desk. No sooner had he finished *The Bolt* than he signed contracts for another four plays, and, besides, he was to complete the music for the variety revue *Killed Conditionally* by Voyevodin and Ryss for Leningrad's music hall. This vaudeville show, featuring the best representatives of the young Soviet art of the revue—the composer Dunayevsky, Utesov's jazz-band show and the singer Shulzhenko—was to help train the population in civil air defense. It closely resembled in style a tasteless potpourri in which the main idea was conveyed in particular by a trained dog, Alma, and circus horses gracefully prancing on the stage. Shostakovich, who had long excelled in knowledge of all the intricacies of this applied medium, easily coped with a few dozen turns. But soon he came to dislike intensely the music he composed for these shows. He could no longer force himself to carry on in this genre.

Dmitry Shostakovich in 1940.

Adulthood

A SECOND OPERA

In mid-November of 1931, Shostakovich sent an article he entitled a "Declaration of Duties of the Composer" to *The Worker and the Theater*, a magazine which had assessed in a negative light most of his compositions. He was depressed and wanted to explain the past. His letter read:

"From the beginning of 1929 to the end of 1931, I have worked as a composer of incidental music. . . . It is an open secret that now, at the time of the 14th anniversary of the October Revolution, the situation on the musical front is catastrophic. . . . I am profoundly convinced that it is precisely the exodus of composers to the theater that is responsible for this situation. . . . Music there performs the function of accentuating 'despair' or 'delight.' There are certain standard tricks in that music: a strike on the drums to announce the entrance of a new character, the 'cheerful and fiery' dance of positive characters, a foxtrot for degradation, and cheerful music for a happy finale. Such is the material for the composer's art. It is a crime against Soviet music to reduce its role to adaptation to the taste and artistic method of the theater. . . . It is in fact depersonalization of the composer. As far as Soviet musical productions are concerned, we have witnessed some abominable specimens here (*The Red Poppy, Ice and Steel, The Bolt, The Golden Age.* . . .). All these were created in close collaboration with the theater. The result is a disgrace. . . .

"Let me sum up. We must do away with depersonalization of the composer. . . . It is with a heavy heart that I reaffirm my commitment to the Vakhtangov Theater to write the music for *Hamlet*. As for *The Negro* and *Concrete Hardens*, I declare my intention to cancel my contracts in a few days. I am no longer able to depersonalize myself and fabricate cliché music. In this way I will clear the obstacles to my plan to write a large symphony dedicated to the fifteenth anniversary of the October Revolution. . . ."

Dmitry Shostakovich, "Declaration of Duties of the Composer," *The Worker and the Theater*, 1931, No. 31.

At the time when Shostakovich felt mature enough to come up with his declaration of principles and attempt a serious assessment of his successes and setbacks he was 25. His record was sad in his own view. Of all his compositions of the last few years, perhaps only the First Symphony was recognized without reservations. An indignant majority had opposed the avant-garde First Piano Sonata, *Aphorisms* and *The Nose*. Disparaging remarks were made now and then about his Second and Third Symphonies. Both his ballets were ignominious failures. His motion-picture music had too many opponents, too. To cap it all, a week before he wrote "Declaration," the premiere of *The Golden Mountains* in Moscow was interrupted by a power outage. The music for the film had nothing to do with that incident, of course, but it was a vexing addition to the long and bitter chain of setbacks. As for his recent work in the dramatic theater, which he regarded as a dubious episode in his life, it was precisely this work that he was praised for as an example to follow.

> "After *The Nose*, Shostakovich has much more closely approached a solution to the problem of Soviet opera by writing the music for *The Shot*. In this play ... the music forms are far more flexible, more innovative and much more in harmony with the themes of the play, which are topical Soviet themes."
>
> *The Worker and the Theater*, 1930, No. 7.

Shostakovich's relations with RAPM were strained. His innovative ideas did not fit the narrow framework of its declared guidelines and were too often at variance with the leading trends in its artistic activities. He was not attracted by the immediate rewards of the "promising" musical genres. Accusations of formalism made him apprehensive but carried no weight.

When *The Worker and the Theater* responded to his "Declaration" with M. Yankovsky's open letter, "Who Is Against? All," Shostakovich evaded a polemic. He seemed not to hear accusations of ideological "waverings" and "a confusion of creative ideas." He kept silent. He was unwilling to argue, since he realized only too well that another dispute would simply deepen the rift between him and RAPM. He chose to concentrate on his work.

In March 1932, the premiere of the play *Hamlet* with music by Shostakovich was held at the Vakhtangov Theater. That was his first excursion into the art of the great English poet, the beginning of his "Shakespeareana."

At the same time, he started work on a symphony entitled provisionally *From Karl Marx to Our Day*, which he had mentioned in his "Declaration" as a composition he intended to write for the 15th anniversary of the October Revolution. The symphony was to consist of five movements with a chorus and a solo vocalist. The text was to be made up of material from Karl Marx's life, excerpts from *The Theses on Feuerbach*, and documents on the history of the world revolutionary labor movement. Unfortunately, his plan did not materialize in full, although he had completed the first movement and worked on the text for the other movements in close collaboration with the poet Nikolai Aseyev.

On April 24, 1932, the central organ of the Soviet press, the newspaper *Pravda,* published the resolution of the Central Committee of the Communist Party "On Restructuring Literary and Artistic Organizations," which was a step of fundamental significance for the further development of Soviet literature and art. Shostakovich, who was clearly aware of the necessity and timeliness of this restructuring, described the resolution as a "document of historic importance." At the end of spring he was elected to the first governing board of the newly formed Soviet Composers' Union.

By the time the resolution was published, RAPM's methods of artistic work had completely lost their effectiveness, turning at times into a caricature of themselves. The theory of a mass "song opera" with monumental choral scenes and a hymnic concluding apotheosis had proved untenable. It was high time to depart temporarily from focusing on the collective, communal interpretation of life and to discern in the many-faced athletic crowd the face of every individual. Shostakovich sensed this necessity more keenly than many other members of the artistic community. He was among the pioneers who directed their attention to the lyrical-psychological drama in quests of new ways of developing Soviet opera. On December 17, 1932, he completed his two years' work on *Lady Macbeth of Mtsensk.*

> "The theme developed by Shostakovich with such singular forcefulness and brilliance deals with Russia's past — of Gogol, Sukhovo-Kobylin and Saltykov-Shchedrin, the horrible dead Russia of officialdom and red tape, police brutality and conceited bourgeoisie. This is a grotesque on a par with Swift's and Voltaire's, a veritable indictment. . . . He has come close to great tragic conceptions, to depicting fierce conflicts between world outlooks and passions, to most profound lyricism."
>
> Ivan Sollertinsky, *Shostakovich's Path in Music,* 1934.

Shostakovich had come upon this subject almost by chance. He had discovered in a book shop a new edition of Nikolai Leskov's short novel with illustrations by Boris Kustodiev. He had known them from his youth. Now after the artist's death he recalled them one by one, turning the pages and getting a new insight into the world of a master of pure Russian prose. He suddenly realized that Leskov's short novel contained an exciting theme of gigantic proportions: a theme of all-absorbing love transforming and exalting the human personality.

So the subject had been found. *Lady Macbeth* drew him so deeply into a world of new imagery and captivated him so strongly that he made plans to write later a full opera tetralogy about Russian women.

Shostakovich had formed an idea of the personages of the future opera immediately, even before he started work on the libretto together with Alexander Preis. His progress in composition, however, exposed ever more clearly the glaring discrepancy between the emotional mood of his music and the spirit of Leskov's novel. The composer's purpose to tell of evil deeds and cruelty, deadly passion and the devastating power of love, seemed incongruous with the background of Leskov's detached style of a chronicle. This style was discarded, and the characters were changed. "The victims have turned into executioners, and the murderer has become a victim"—(Sollertinsky). A story of everyday life gave way to a drama, because it contained a wealth of tragic material typical of 19th-century Russian literature.

In his article "My Interpretation of *Lady Macbeth*," Shostakovich gave terse but salient portraits of the characters: Katerina's father-in-law, Boris Timofeyevich, a "dyed-in-the-wool hard-fisted master, a cruel brute who would stop at nothing to achieve his goals"; her husband, Zinovy Borisovich, a miserable good-for-nothing, a veritable "degenerate"; and Katerina's lover, Sergei, "the most vicious criminal one can imagine." These characters are entirely devoid of the slightest trace of "idyllic, satisfied good-naturedness, patriarchal staidness, benevolence and dependability"—(Sollertinsky). The composer's chief concern and object of compassion was the image of Katerina, which he painted in truly tragic colors. It was not accidental that he specifically stated that for him the focus of the conflict lay precisely in the fate of this woman. When Vladimir Nemirovich-Danchenko, the director of the Moscow Art Theater, staged the opera in Moscow, he emphasized this fact by its title: *Katerina Izmailovà.*

In his interpretation of the heroine, Shostakovich was a direct heir to the humanistic traditions of Russian artistic culture, a heir to Nekrasov and Dostoyevsky, Tchaikovsky and Rimsky-Korsakov. His Katerina is one of the most exciting images in Russian and world theater. She belongs to the women who were described by the remarkable theater critic Nikolai Berkovsky in these perspicacious and sympathetic words:

> ". . . It was clear that they were forced to lapse into evil against their will, that they were by no means disposed toward evil. Evil was imposed upon them; they were compelled to resort to evil in self-defense; they committed immoral acts motivated by their injured pride; their shame and despair prodded them to atrocious acts . . ."
>
> Nikolai Berkovsky, *Literature and Theater,* 1969.

Thus, the composer immediately defined for himself the motivating forces in the tragic story of a merchant's wife, Katerina Izmailova. On the one hand, the world of stale provincial life, corruption, hypocrisy, cruelty and lust. On the other hand, Katerina Izmailova, flesh and blood of this world, who nevertheless rose above and rebelled against this world by the force of her passion. The opposite poles were clearly delineated, and the music of the opera revealed the essence of each of them with that vividness of detail and exhaustive veracity which distinguish the work of an artist having perfect mastery of the laws of opera dramaturgy and general symphonic development. The new principles of the arrangement of scenes and new means of expression found in the opera *The Nose* were affirmed and reinforced in *Lady Macbeth of Mtsensk,* with superlative skill and determination.

The composer invoked the full powers of a scathing grotesque and a caustic lampoon to satirize the backwater existence of Mtsensk inhabitants. In his music, vulgarity and meanness sit on the throne, celebrating their hideous festival, and the common genre of thieves' Latin, parodic waltzes and polkas reigns supreme.

Shockingly vulgar and lewd is Sergei, particularly in love scenes with Katerina, who is seized with sincere passion; lustful and vulgar is Boris Timofeyevich, worming his way to his daughter-in-law in the absence of his son; ugly and dissolute are the menials and shopmen jeering at the awkward female cook; the policemen who personify power and supreme order behave as lascivious boors. Even the priest bending over the dead body of Boris Timofeyevich, who was poisoned by Katerina, sings vulgar couplets.

On this background the truly human pain of the music is agonizing, and the startling beauty of the impassioned melodies the composer devotes to Katerina is poignant and strange. The lofty lyricism of the opera and its vivid, inspired humanism are associated exclusively with the character of Katerina.

> "I have composed this opera on a tragic plane. I believe that *Lady Macbeth* might be classified as a tragisatirical opera. Although Katerina is a murderer who has killed her husband and father-in-law, I feel compassion for her. I tried to lend sombre satircal colors to her milieu . . . to produce a sharp-pointed satire unmasking hypocrites and arousing hatred of the frightful tyranny and humiliation of life in a merchant family."
>
> Dmitry Shostakovich, "Tragedy-Satire," *Sovietskoye Iskusstvo* (Soviet Art), 16 October 1932.

A tragedy-satire. That was a new chapter in the history of Russian opera, another milestone in Shostakovich's art. After *The Nose,* an opera-masque in which humor was the keynote and buffoonery the chief style of performance, the composer turned to psychological realism and created an opera in which the fusion of aesthetically antipodal principles gives birth to a new artistic quality. The grotesque in *Lady Macbeth* is gloomy and sinister and is devoid of even a trace of that bitter yet comical spirit which prevails in *The Nose*. In the lyrical episodes, Shostakovich for the first time expressed himself with frank pathos and presented the melodic wealth of Russian songs with great profundity and forcefulness.

> "When the nightmarish, oppressive atmosphere of Katerina's humdrum life is disturbed by her quiet, weirdly concentrated talking to herself, the music attains its supreme qualities: humaneness, emotional veracity, the highest intensity of suffering. Katerina's monologues are perhaps the finest pages in the opera. . . .

Despite his great dedication to his work, Shostakovich could always find time for enjoying the outdoors and even for sports, especially tennis.

Opposite:
In the winter of 1932, Shostakovich married research scientist Nina Varzar.

"The composer has depicted her image in a gentle, lyrical light. This imparts to his music a valuable novel quality which lurked in the background until now: melodiousness, motif development and warmth as well as feminine tenderness."

Boris Asafiev, *Shostakovich's Music and the Opera* Lady Macbeth of Mtsensk, 1934.

The opening pages of the opera are colored in warm tones unusual for Shostakovich: the intonations of Katerina's initial monologue are plaintively wistful though full of anxiety, and her melancholy arioso romance, "The Ant Dragging a Straw," unfolds with flowing smoothness.

A phrase in the arioso broken off on a helpless note opens, according to the law of classical drama, the first conflict between the antagonistic forces ("Shall we have mushrooms today?" Boris Timofeyevich asks in a tone of command), and the action vigorously gains speed and moves toward the general climax in the final scene. As the colors of the devastating grotesque grow brighter (the climax of this theme is the outrageously cynical scene of the affair between Sergei and Sonetka in the finale), Katerina's lyrical image is thrown into an ever more salient relief. Shostakovich transforms this image from one consumed with boredom of inaction and subdued hatred ("You shall!" she responds to Boris Timofeyevich in a hollow voice) into one of affection and humaneness and, finally, leads it to an agonizing spiritual breakdown. Her role acquires "amazing realism of intonation . . ., and tragic colors reminiscent more of Shakespeare than of Leskov" (Sollertinsky).

In the finale, when Katerina, exhausted by her anguish and despair, begins to sing almost inaudibly, as if half asleep, of a "lone lake in the woods," the music reaches the summit of epic generalization. Her song echoes the song chanted by convicts clanking their chains on an endless Siberian road. Just as the opera *The Nose* may be considered an heir to Rimsky-Korsakov's *The Golden Cockerel*, Shostakovich's second opera may be considered an heir to Modest Moussorgsky's people's dramas.

Lady Macbeth of Mtsensk, completed in December 1932, was to be produced by two theaters: Leningrad's MALEGOT and Moscow's Nemirovich-Danchenko Musical Theater. Both companies got down to work on the production with great enthusiasm.

At MALEGOT *Lady Macbeth* was interpreted as social satire, and its production emphasized and added sharpness to the grotesque essence of Shostakovich's music. There was full unanimity in the theater as far as the merits of the opera were concerned. The director Samuil Samosud expressed the general opinion in this phrase: "An opera which makes an epoch." The right of participation in the production was a coveted goal of many.

In Moscow the opera was interpreted in the spirit of the Stanislavsky school as a realistic tragedy, and its grotesque line was played down. The production was directed by Nemirovich-Danchenko. Rumors of Shostakovich's new opera quickly spread within the musical community; those who had attended rehearsals hastened to share their impressions with others.

> "Since your departure, another great musical event has taken place here: an orchestral rehearsal of Shostakovich's opera *Lady Macbeth of Mtsensk*. The music was stunningly good although painful to listen to at places. The orchestration was equally unusual. . . ."
>
> Excerpt from a letter by N. Myaskovsky to Sergei Prokofiev, July 21, 1933.

Lady Macbeth of Mtsensk had its first night in Leningrad on January 22, 1934. Its production in Moscow on January 24, 1934, added to the sensational success of the premiere.

The heavy curtains of velvet slowly draw apart, rustling softly, and Katerina's first cue, uttered in a toneless voice, falls into the silence of the audience. "Oh, life is such a bore! I wish I were dead." Life, indeed, is dull, torpid and stifling in the Izmailovs' home, and Katerina's confession of her hatred of this life is gloomy and sad. After seeing her husband, a man she detests, to the flour mill, she aimlessly shuffles across the courtyard with a look of despair on her face.

Further events develop in rapid succession: Katerina's first meeting with Sergei, her first assignation with her beloved, the poisoning of her father-in-law, the murder of her husband, the wedding, her arrest, and the last conversation between her and Sergei.

With the unerring intuition of a mature dramaturgist and symphonist, Shostakovich lines up the nine scenes of the opera in a coherent whole, linking them together by numerous intonational threads, developing the action in symphonic interludes and skillfully preparing tense culminations by orchestral means. The opera immediately and firmly grips the attention of the audience and keeps it spellbound to the end.

> "I went to Shostakovich's *Lady Macbeth* and was greatly impressed. Nemirovich-Danchenko's production is excellent. It's simple, without tricks or extravagant details. A genuine human drama. Shostakovich is a genius."
>
> Entry in Alexander Goldenweiser's diary, January 28, 1934.

Both premieres became a veritable festival of Soviet opera art. The composer was showered with congratulations. The press was replete with delighted headlines. Discussions about the opera flared up within musical circles, but all were in agreement about its superlative merits. *Lady Macbeth* immediately became the most popular opera on the repertoire of the season in both Leningrad and Moscow.

> "Shostakovich's new opera is indisputably one of the most significant events in Soviet musical and theatrical life. This is, in effect, the first large, truly talented and remarkably masterful work of opera art in the 16 years since the October Revolution."
>
> *Sovietskoye Iskusstvo* (Soviet Art), February 11, 1934.

Sovfoto

DMITRI SHOSTAKOVICH

The composer at work.

The Third Ballet

While he was busy composing *Lady Macbeth,* Shostakovich performed in public as a pianist quite rarely, if at all. His ambitious plans left him with no time for guest tours or for preparing his repertoire at home, and, most important of all, he found it rather hard to combine the study of another composer's music with his own music, which absorbed him entirely. Moreover, he wrote no piano music of his own in those years.

As soon as the opera was completed, however, Shostakovich returned to the piano and composed with skillful ease his 24 preludes and First Piano Concerto, the latter with special pleasure. Perhaps he was tired of the strain of the last few years and longed for a changeover to a different emotional sphere, or perhaps he simply wanted to try his hand, in his own and again innovative way, in a genre with which he had not dealt before. Whatever his motive, the concerto he had composed was dynamic and mischievous, even with a touch of bravado, and was interspersed with intonations from Beethoven, Haydn, Mahler and Weber. His was a teasing and good-natured "challenge" to the conservatism and seriousness of the classical concerto. It was a conflict between the present and the past, and the composer's youth, strength, talent and exuberant imagination asserted themselves in such unexpected and demonstrative collisions.

The Concerto bore an imprint of his experience in the ballet and the applied arts. Its bustling and impetuous music, as though guided by an invisible conductor, narrated what was going on with the expressiveness of a gesture or mimicry. It rushed from one theme to another, stopping in the middle of a sentence; it mixed solemnity with buffoonery; it leaped from the fanfare of a summoning trumpet to the poetry of a waltz and the intimacy of a fox-trot; it hurled the bold rhythms of a galop into the atmosphere of calm reflection. It seethed with life like a gurgling spring, and it sparkled with humor without reverence for time-honored traditions.

When posters announced the premiere of the Concerto, to be held on October 15, 1933, Shostakovich was glad to come on the stage, and he played his First Piano Concerto with the same ingenuity and extravagance he had displayed in composing it.

The Cello Sonata, which he wrote a year later—austere, serious and profoundly lyrical—stood in sharp contrast to the Concerto. And again he did not authorize another musician to take over the premiere but played the sonata himself in concert with the cellist Kubatsky.

In the spring of 1935, Shostakovich went to Turkey with a group of performers. The representative delegation, which included the renowned violinist David Oistrakh, Lev Oborin, Barsova, Maksakova and Pirogov, was to introduce Soviet music to foreign audiences. In addition, the guest performances of Soviet good-will envoys were of enormous political significance in view of the tense situation taking shape in the world.

When he was leaving on his guest tour, Shostakovich already knew that rehearsals of his third ballet, *The Limpid Stream*, were in progress at MALEGOT. The librettists were Fedor Lopukhov and Adrian Piotrovsky, the production was directed by Lopukhov, Mikhail Bobyshev was invited to design the scenery, and Pavel Feldt, Shostakovich's close friend of the Conservatory years and the composers' circle, was to be the conductor.

The year 1935 was one of great uplift. The country had fulfilled the First Five-Year Plan ahead of schedule and was working enthusiastically to attain the targets of the Second Five-Year Plan. The transition of life to new, socialist principles was being completed in the rural areas. At that stage the collective-farm theme seemed the most topical and necessary.

> "We wanted to produce a gala ballet pervaded with gaiety, the joy of life and a youthful spirit. This led us to the socialist village, to a collective farm . . . We do not think that the joy of labor can be shown on the stage only by imitating the so-called 'production motions.' Indeed, a merry and festive dance of young collective farmers can give a truer-to-life picture of the joy of work under socialism than imitation of the movements of people manning threshing machines or harvesting combines . . ."
>
> Fedor Lopukhov, Adrian Piotrovsky, *The Limpid Stream*, 1935.

The production team worked on the ballet with extraordinary zeal, straining to identify as quickly and as unmistakably as possible the right path which had eluded them in their earlier experiments. They sought to create a production free from false enthusiasm, ostentatious dramatization and declarative conflicts. At the same time, this was to be a truly choreographic performance, since they believed, unlike many others of their ilk, in the powerful appeal of the immortal language of the dance and intended to instill their faith into their future audiences.

> "The authors wish to demonstrate to the public the immense possibilities of Soviet ballet, in which 'The Limpid Stream' is just one of the first few attempts, courageous even if naïve and somewhat awkward."
>
> *Ibid.*

They produced a comedy. The libretto tells of some amusing episodes in the life of a collective-farm agronomist who takes a fancy to a ballerina visiting his village on a guest tour. Little does he know that his own wife is an ex-ballerina who can satisfy her husband's passion for the lofty art just as well as a Moscow star. There is a whirlwind of events which involves an eccentric tourist and virtuous young collective farmers, while the visiting ballerina is discovered to be an old friend of the agronomist's wife. They jointly teach a lesson to the unfortunate lady-killer. The final scene is one of a holiday harvest dance in which the agronomist and his wife perform solo parts to the background of a *corps de ballet*.

The libretto was far from perfect. So after the premiere held on April 4, 1935, the reviewers were unsparing in their satirical comments. They reproached the ballet, not without reason, for its overemphasis on divertissement, and Sollertinsky was absolutely right in his insistence on "a life-like, coherent action and life-like characters." Inspired by the achievements of the Soviet dramatic theater, literature and poetry, critics expected such achievements to be immediately made in ballet as well, which was impossible by virtue of the simple and objective laws of artistic creation. That pioneering ballet on a collective farm theme could not have been anything but a "continuous three-act divertissement" in which the spontaneity of the dance had nevertheless ousted pantomime and physical exercises.

Shostakovich's music was comprised, in accordance with the logic of the libretto, of a series of internally complete and independent parts. He had even borrowed for *The Limpid Stream* episodes from the music for *The Golden Age* and *The Bolt* without attempting to integrate the mosaic of numbers with a common dramaturgical idea. He sensed perfectly the divertissement nature of the ballet and was unwilling to disturb it with symphonic elements alien to it.

The music, it is true, was not as good as in his first ballets. It lacked the forceful populist message of *The Bolt* and offered no special opportunities for developing a grotesque satirical theme. Nevertheless, critics pointed out a sanguine and cheerful wave in Shostakovich's music, its force and dynamism maintaining the action without a respite through a distinctive series of numbers. At any rate, the ballet proved more viable than the early experiments in this genre. In short, full credit for its success was due to Shostakovich's music and the brilliant dances devised by Lopukhov. The audience forgot about the flaws of the libretto and instead were captivated by the ballet master's imagination and the plasticity and expressiveness of the classical choreography.

Before long, *The Limpid Stream* was staged at the Bolshoi in Moscow. Lopukhov was invited as director, Yuri Fayer was the conductor, and the scenery and costumes were designed by Vladimir Dmitriyev. The ballet fascinated the audience, although the divertissement nature and far-fetchedness of the plot were even more strikingly expressed in this production. Shostakovich's music, however, sparkled with new colors as Yuri Fayer emphasized its choreographical nature to lend it refinement and gracefulness.

"In this production, Shostakovich's music is truly choreographic—but not in the ordinary sense. With extraordinary forcefulness and temperament, it guides the action throughout the performance, imparting harmony to movement and an exalted cheerful tone to the ballet as a whole, and fills it with tremendous dynamism and sincere joy. Its vigorous sounds give one an almost tactile sensation of modern life."

Rabochaya Moskva (Moscow Worker), December 2, 1935.

In this choreographic comedy on a modern theme, the classical dance made a comeback on the stage. That was the key task facing the composer and the choreographer, and they accomplished it brilliantly. For all that, however, *The Limpid Stream* was destined to live a short life on the stage, sharing the fate of *The Golden Age* and *The Bolt,* the opinions of the critics notwithstanding. In a series of experiments extending over a period of three decades, Shostakovich's ballets were only three among many others, although more successful than most. The art of ballet advanced by giant strides, and these memorable and instructive events in music remain milestones on this path.

Two articles published early in 1936 came as a surprise to many. The first one, headlined "Muddle Instead of Music," appeared on January 27 and criticized *Lady Macbeth of Mtsensk.* The composer was accused of "extreme formalism," "crude naturalism," and "melodic poverty." Ten days later, on February 6, another article entitled "A Ballet Fraud" and denouncing *The Limpid Stream* was printed in the press. This time Shostakovich was criticized for a "bucolic portrayal" of real life and a formalistic approach to folklore. Both the opera and the ballet were dropped from the repertoire.

The charges against the composer, whose art was in many ways ahead of its time, would eventually be proved groundless. Years would go by, the complex formative stage of Soviet ballet would lose its hyperbolic, painful acuity and recede into the past, and *The Limpid Stream* would occupy its rightful place in the repertoire. The opera *Lady Macbeth of Mtsensk* would be born anew for a long life on the stage.

For the time being, though, Shostakovich was going ahead with his work. The composition of his new Fourth Symphony was nearing completion. Its first sketches had been made in 1934, and the composer described it as "the credo of my music."

A Symphonic Trilogy

"Dear Ronya,

"I have nearly completed my symphony. Now I am orchestrating the finale (third movement). As soon as I am through . . . I will come to Moscow to show it to you and someone else. I am in a sour mood and have no idea of what to do next. This is why I am taking my time about finishing the symphony."

Excerpt from a letter by Dmitry Shostakovich to composer Vissarion Shebalin, April 17, 1936.

In May 1936, Shostakovich finally completed his work of two years on the Fourth Symphony and brought it to Moscow to play it to his closest friends, to hear their comments and to regain his self-confidence. The latter was perhaps most important of all.

In Moscow the symphony was received with delight, and on returning home the composer handed over the score to Fritz Stiedry, chief conductor of the Leningrad Philharmonic. Rehearsals were soon started. At the last minute, however, the premiere had to be cancelled. The symphony remained unknown until it was performed in public a quarter century later, in December 1961.

In 1937 Shostakovich completed his Fifth Symphony and after another two years, his Sixth. The composer's interests clearly gravitated toward a large symphony, and the Fourth had proved to be the threshold beyond which Shostakovich reached maturity as a symphonist.

In the early 1930's, Soviet symphonic music was in the throes of another crisis of growth, which was strikingly evident in the discussion on its problems sponsored by the USSR Composers' Union in 1935. These were problems of vital importance and demanded an immediate debate on a national scale.

One of the questions at issue was the content of music. It was mandatory to decide once and for all whether a Soviet symphony should be filled with conflict and openly dramatic and to what extent it should rely on a program, whether it could be an optimistic tragedy, though without emasculated optimism, embellishments and ostentation. Sollertinsky's extremist argument was that "the form of the four-movement classical symphony as a genre, as a musical scheme, had long disintegrated."

Zhizn Iskusstva (The Life of Art), 1929, No. 45.

He expressed one of the most radical viewpoints, but it was shared by many, and Soviet symphonic music was shaking in a fever of experiments and quests in the field of form.

Composers made their best achievements in the field of program music. Shostakovich himself contributed to it by his second and third symphonies. A series of dramatic symphonies were composed: *Lenin* by Shebalin; *A Collective-Farm Symphony* by Myaskovsky; the symphonic dithyramb "The USSR: Vanguard of the World Proletariat" by Krein; *Turksib (Turkistan-Siberian Railway)* by Steinberg; *The Arctic Symphony* by Vasilenko; *The Izhora Symphony* by Shcherbachev. It was time composers came up with a philosophical interpretation of reality and its burning problems, but works of "pure," nonprogram, symphonic music swerved from this goal one way or another and lapsed into a monumental and grandiloquent tone. Shostakovich was one of the trailblazers who led symphonic music out of its crisis.

Shostakovich had collected enough material. He had a record of work in all genres of musical art: the cinema and the theater, opera and ballet, vocal and instrumental music. He had passed through the temptations of programmed music and formal convention, left behind the rigidity and placard-like declarativeness of *Dedication to October*, the songlike melodiousness of *May Day* and experiments with the spoken word and form, to return to what he had started in his First Symphony—a purely instrumental composition of several movements. Enriched with knowledge and experience, Shostakovich now rose to a qualitatively new level of thinking as a symphonist capable of a profound analysis of his life experience, a serious presentation of civic themes common to all mankind and their comprehensive elucidation, and a refined artistic generalization. Shostakovich's trilogy proved to be a classical example, perhaps without peer in Soviet music, of the tragic and lyric-psychological symphonic form. The gem of the trilogy was the Fifth Symphony.

His path toward the new type of symphony lay through the theater—the forcefulness and veracity of the characters in *Lady Macbeth of Mtsensk*, the multiple and lifelike stage colossals, the principles of symphonic dramaturgy and the means of expression found in the opera. He arrived at the interpretation of the symphonic form as action on many different planes where the laws of nature and the laws of human life are equally inexorable, where the truth, however bitter, is revealed at the cost of a tense struggle without compromise or reconciliation. Victory and defeat are equally possible. Even in the most catastrophical situations and in the nethermost depths of despair, however, faith in the consummate beauty of human reason and spirit prevails. This is the mainspring of the lofty humanism of Shostakovich's music, the optimistic principle of his most tragic symphonic canvases, the Shakespearean vein in his art.

The theme of the evolution of the human personality which the composer had defined for himself imperatively asserted itself in his art, lending it a civic and political content and a philosophical, ethical message. The problems "man and humanity" and "man and his time" became the pivotal themes of his music.

Shostakovich's music was discovered to have evolutional links with the art of Bach, Beethoven, Tchaikovsky and Mahler. The classical sources of his art were fully and graphically revealed not as imitation or borrowing but as allegiance to the lofty humanistic and aesthetic ideals of the past, as an embodiment of the entire wealth of the classical heritage at a new, modern stage.

The composer's musical language was also undergoing changes. His means of expression grew simpler and more austere, his melodic patterns were becoming more elastic and flexible, all that was superfluous and exaggeratedly rigid was vanishing to make way for a crystallizing, ideal equilibrium between reason and emotion, and profound concentrated meditation and dramatic intensity of feeling.

The Fourth Symphony, which was a turning point in Shostakovich's art, is his most impassioned and intense for the sincerity and integrity of its subjective expression. Never before had Shostakovich's music been so tragic or conveyed such excruciating anguish and suffering.

In search of truth, the human who is torn by contradictions flings himself from one support to another, comes upon cruelty, coarseness and vulgarity, shrinks back in horror, rushes forward again and finally collapses in utter exhaustion. Such is the first act of the drama. The second act brings no relief. The swift dynamic motion befogs the mind with ghostly and sarcastic images. The final act is a funeral march. The solemn and mournful procession passes through a polka, waltzes, a galop and a song, as if through a series of almost unreal images, and finally reaches a coda full of deep sorrow. This is exhaustion but not humility.

There is a concept in musicology known as the problem of the finale. The finale of a composition is a criterion of its author's maturity and mastery, his attitude to himself and to his time, as the conclusion summing up all that he has experienced and expressed. The finale of the Fourth Symphony is tragic, but this tragedy is exalted and full of wisdom.

After *Lady Macbeth,* Shostakovich's turn towards the lyrical, tragic pathos of the Fourth Symphony was legitimate and natural. The striking expressiveness, impulsiveness and throbbing anxiety of this music were a specific protest against and a challenge to impersonal placard-like music. Shostakovich claimed his right to speak the language of lofty tragedy, assertig it with the sincerity and passion of an artist deeply concerned about the destiny of Soviet art.

In 1937 Shostakovich completed his Fifth Symphony, which is justly regarded as the first Soviet symphonic classic. For the general public, who had not yet heard the Fourth Symphony, the Fifth appeared shortly after the ballet *The Limpid Stream.* It was

Shostakovich plays the piano part in a performance of his First Piano Concerto at the Grand Hall of the Moscow Conservatory, with Stolerov conducting.

significant that the article in which Shostakovich announced his new symphony was entitled "My Answer in Music."

> ". . The theme of my symphony is the assertion of the human personality. It was precisely the human being that I saw in the focus of the conception of my composition, which is lyrical from beginning to end."
>
> Dmitry Shostakovich "My Answer in Music," *Vechernyaya Moskva (Moscow Evening News),* January 25, 1938.

It was a tragedy. A struggle and despair, wrath and determination. But the hero has reached manhood. The strict discipline of thought restrains his feelings and guides them along the sole correct course. Strained reflection does not hasten action. But when the evil of inhumanity in the image of a mechanistic march advances as a stupid and blind force ready to wipe out all life and all that is human, then reason and feelings rise in arms against it.

The Fifth Symphony is classical in every sense of the word. For the first time since Shostakovich's First Symphony it restores the traditional sequence of the four movements of the cycle. It resurrects Beethoven's heroic action and Bach's philosophic concentration. It embodies the classical idea in a new development of the history of culture "through struggle toward victory," "through trials to the stars." It charms one by the classical perfection and completeness of all lines, all forms, all proportions, rising as a graphically simple and austere obelisk to human courage.

And, most important, the music of the finale, energetic and anxious, aspires through the painful efforts of the entire mass of sounds toward the final, victorious note achieving at last its goal in the concluding triumphant sounds of the brass. The finale is not exaltation of victory itself but the achievement of victory.

The public welcomed Shostakovich's Fifth Symphony with tremendous enthusiasm. Their sentiment was summed up by playwright Alexander Afinogenov:

> ". . . We heard Shostakovich's Fifth Symphony. I understand what [Alexei] Tolstoy means in writing that the audience rose in response to this continuous appeal . . . There was a storm of applause, a roar of delight, shouts of 'Hurrah!' Genuine art is celebrating its triumph; this triumph is a challenge to all who believe that Dunayevsky cannot be excelled, that Lebedev-Kumach is the pinnacle of Soviet poetry, and that the song is its only genre. It has come at last: the radiant dawn of the socialist symphony in which one keenly feels a new vision of the world, a new listening perception. Our demonstrations in Red Square, our enthusiasm and our joy are all heard in the organization of sounds, in the unusual reverberation of rolling waves, in the summons of trumpets and the singing of the strings!"
>
> Entry in Alexander Afinogenov's diary, January 29, 1938.

The Fifth Symphony was first performed in Leningrad on November 21, 1937, under the baton of Eugene Mravinsky. That was the first joint work of the composer and the conductor, and it set the stage for their lifelong creative collaboration. Mravinsky would be the first to conduct most of Shostakovich's later symphonies. The composer had found a like-minded comrade and friend.

In the autumn of 1937, Shostakovich joined the faculty of the Leningrad Conservatory at first as a teacher of the orchestration class and a little later of the composition class.

As a teacher, Shostakovich was as loyal to his principles as he was in his art. He was honest, straightforward and firm. He was intolerant of perfunctoriness and dilettantism and tried to inculcate in his students a striving for precision in thinking, for accuracy and for conscientiousness in work. Raised in the academic traditions of Steinberg's school, the composer regarded solid professional training as the basis without which the lofty and inspired art of music was inconceivable. He devoted all his talents as a teacher to this work and raised a splendid galaxy of Soviet master musicians. Among his many gifted students were Georgy Sviridov, Kara Karayev, Boris Chaikovsky, Yuri Levitin and Gherman Galynin.

> "It is very difficult to write about Shostakovich as a teacher . . . He was one of our 'unobtrusive' professors, so to speak—no dogmas; no stereotyped principles; brief remarks, sometimes sharp and picturesque, but usually mild and seemingly incidental. However, they sank deeply into the mind of a responsive student to grow in time into what was incomparably greater: principles, convictions, and taste."
>
> Yuri Levitin, *The Teacher*, 1976.

In 1939 Shostakovich had the title of professor of composition bestowed upon him. He would continue teaching at the Moscow and Leningrad Conservatoires for decades with short breaks. He would play a lot in piano duets and double duets with his students, analyze jointly with them an enormous amount of various kind of music; he would crack jokes, argue, accept defeat, and argue again in defense of his views.

On November 20, 1938, the newspaper *Sovietskoye Iskusstvo (Soviet Art)* featured a brief item under the heading "A Symphony in Memory of Lenin." In it Shostakovich set forth the plan of his new symphony, a composition in four movements with a chorus and soloists based on verses by Vladimir Mayakovsky, Jambul and Stalsky. He worked on the symphony for almost a year. The musical community had expected a monumental and heroic composition of epic scope and hymnic sonority in the final apotheosis. What was heard at its premiere on November 5, 1939, however, had not been expected by anybody. The audience was embarrassed and surprised.

It is hard to tell with assurance now what had interfered with the completion of his plan. We speak of "completion" because some material had obviously been written, and it had determined, by all indications, the mournful character of the first movement of the Sixth Symphony. It is not unlikely that Shostakovich, just like ten-odd years earlier, sensed again the inadequacy of his experience in life and art for the resolution of a theme of such gigantic proportions. It is equally probable that after the Fourth and Fifth symphonies, which summed up all that he had learned over the long years of his creative quests, the composer needed some lead time in which to review his record in composition and to search for new means of expression. He had experienced something like that after composing *Lady Macbeth* and would again need a period of retrospective analysis after the Seventh and Eighth symphonies.

After completing the Fifth Symphony, Shostakovich produced no large compositions for a long time. The year 1938 was one of intensive work on the films *The Vyborg District, Friends, The Great Citizen,* Part One, and *A Man With a Rifle.* The composer switched over enthusiastically to his mass and most *democratic genre* and wrote music brimming with *revolutionary* songs, marches, and the restless noises of streets and squares.

Whether or not it was accidental that all his film opuses were closely associated with the theme of revolution is a matter of guesswork. It is true Shostakovich never departed from revolutionary romanticism in film music for long *(Maxim's Youth, Girlfriends,* 1935; *Maxim Returns, Volochayevka Days,* 1937), but it was precisely in the period of his reflection on the Sixth Symphony that he composed music for these films in rapid succession.

At the same time, Shostakovich turned to what was a totally unfamiliar genre, the quartet.

> "For a full year after submitting the Fifth Symphony, I composed almost nothing. I wrote only a quartet consisting of four short movements. I started to write it without any guiding ideas or feelings, and I thought that nothing would come of it. Indeed, the quartet is one of the most difficult musical genres. I wrote the first page as a peculiar exercise in quartet form without intending to complete and publish it some day . . . Later, however, I became fascinated with my work on the quartet, and I wrote it extremely fast. One should not seek special profundity in this first quartet opus of mine. Its mood is joyful, merry and lyrical. I would like to call it 'Springtime.' "
>
> Dmitry Shostakovich. Excerpt from an *Izvestia* interview, September 29, 1938.

Quite unexpectedly for Shostakovich himself, he gained quite a lot from his first experiment in the quartet genre: the habit of work in a new form and an ability to dispose wisely and sparingly only four performers in a large composition, leaving none of them in the background. What was important, this experiment opened his eyes to a world of objective lyricism, light and cheerful, transparent and crystal clear precisely by virtue of the chamber character of the genre.

Incidental music for four films and one string quartet composed over a fairly long period were a modest achievement, of course. In Shostakovich's art, however, these compositions marked a turning point. His work on them would have been impossible without his actively assimilating the wealth of intonations of the revolutionary era, without his inventing ever more vivid musical means of expression, without his tapping the field of objective lyrical emotions. The composer brilliantly coped with these new tasks.

At last the Sixth Symphony promised by the composer was ready. The first thing that surprised the public was the absence of a chorus of soloists and of any program whatsoever, not to speak of a poetical text. Only three movements were left of the four originally conceived. The glib-tongued critics immediately dubbed the Sixth a "decapitated symphony," clearly hinting at the absence of a first movement, the dynamic and dramatic opening sonata allegro. Shostakovich seemed to have resumed experimenting with the symphonic form which he had but recently sculptured so perfectly in the Fifth Symphony.

The epic largo of the symphony, pervaded with intonations of workers' and revolutionary songs, develops in the movement of a mournful mass procession—the rustle of footsteps, the flutter of lowered flags, subdued voices, bitter exclamations and mournful silence. The largo resembles most of all the scene of a funereal meeting or, rather, an episode in a film where each mourner delivers his "funeral oration." These are the voices of many who have come to life in the memory of one, an artist who is a patriot of his country and a chronicler of its history.

The subsequent movements of the symphony are two chamber scherzos. The first of them spills in dynamic and iridescent, and at times slightly restless, motion. This scherzo's swift flight reminds one of an old fairy tale about omnipresent gnomes. The finale, sparkling with gaiety (without parodic imitation or deliberate mockery), reproduces the charming spirit of the urban music of the '30s: the awkward sounds of Luna-park brass bands, the lightness of polkas and waltzes, the carefree tunes of young people's songs. In some elusive features, the finale resembles now the simple-hearted divertimenti of Haydn and Mozart, and now the careless gracefulness of Schubert's waltzes.

The last composition of the trilogy, a symphonic scherzo inspired with civic lyricism and overcoming subjective emotions through a profound realization of the supreme value of life, provides a brilliant answer to all the tormenting questions of the Fourth Symphony.

In 1940, at the request of the members of the Beethoven Quartet, Shostakovich wrote the Piano Quintet, which was an extension of the Sixth Symphony, as if its images were conveyed to the pages of transparent chamber music to become even more flexible and natural.

"What is the novelty and appeal of this composition?

The quintet is made up of a series of lyrical, humanly truthful moods and images. It enthralls the listener with its depth and magnificence. Shostakovich has found a lyrical solution to the key artistic problem of today: he presents a truthful, sincere and inspired revelation of the spiritual wealth of the human personality . . . The aesthetic impact and musical expressiveness of the quintet are truly irresistible."

Pravda, November 25, 1940.

The quintet became the gem of the Fourth Soviet Ten-Day Music Festival and was hailed in the press as the best composition of the year. When the first U.S.S.R. State Prizes were announced in 1941, Shostakovich was awarded a first-degree prize for his quintet.

While he was still at work on his quintet, Shostakovich undertook to produce a new edition of Moussorgsky's opera *Boris Godunov* at the request of the Bolshoi, which was planning to put it back on its repertoire.

"I revere Moussorgsky as the greatest of Russian composers. My task was to penetrate as deeply as possible into the original creative conception of that genius of music, to develop that conception and convey it to the audience."

Dmitry Shostakovich, "The Opera Score," *Izvestia,* May 1, 1941.

Shostakovich would admit later that his work on the opera caused him a lot of worry. He had to study scrupulously Moussorgsky's autographs and drafts, to restore what had been thought to be irretrievably lost, and to find unmistakably correct solutions, relying exclusively on his own knowledge of Moussorgsky's style and language. Moreover, any revision, however slight, in the first edition made by Rimsky-Korsakov, an acknowledged master of orchestration, demanded extreme caution and tact.

Shostakovich's instrumentation of *Boris Godunov* was his first penetration into the innermost depths of Moussorgsky's art. In 1959 he would make a new musical edition of *Khovanshchina* and three years later an instrumentation of Moussorgsky's vocal cycle *Songs and Dances of Death.* With this work he would infinitely enrich his own art.

The Tocsin of War

THE LENINGRAD SYMPHONY

June 22, 1941, the day of Nazi Germany's attack on the U.S.S.R., found Shostakovich in Leningrad, a professor at the Leningrad Conservatory. On the same day, he volunteered to join the Red Army. His request was denied. After a month, he applied for enlistment in the home guard and was turned down again. He was beside himself with anger. A little later he submitted a third application, and in response was offered the chance to evacuate with his family to a safe area. His answer was a resolute "No!"

Leningrad was a front-line city from the early days of the war, and the members of its artistic community rallied to its defense. They continued to work in the theaters and museums, on the concert stage and in studios. They were not in the firing lines in the literal sense, but their work was part and parcel of the country's war effort.

> "The time of the Great Patriotic War was one of a tremendous patriotic and, I would say, creative uplift among Soviet composers. They wrote a vast number of compositions on patriotic themes, on themes of love of the motherland and hatred of its enemies. In the early period of the war, many songs and works in the minor genres were composed: marching songs, ditties, sometimes in a humorous vein, music for variety shows. That was the composers' prompt response to the dramatic, daily events of wartime."
>
> Dmitry Shostakovich, "Soviet Music in Wartime," 1944. Excerpt from a report to a plenary meeting of the Organizing Committee of the Soviet Composers' Union.

These events dictated the need for an immediate reorganization of all cultural work in the country, and the speed with which all Soviet art found the correct, populist tone to meet the exigencies of the situation deserves admiration. On June 23, *Pravda* published Surkov's poem "Our Oath Is Victory," and on June 24 *Izvestia* appeared with Lebedev-Kumach's "The Holy War." On the evening of June 26, the song "The Holy War," composed by A.V. Alexandrov, was performed for the first time during the send-off ceremony at Moscow's Byelorussian Terminal for troops going to the front lines. On June 28, the first wartime issue of the *Boyevoi Karandash (Fighting Pencil),* the illustrated magazine of the Soviet Artists' Union, came out in Leningrad. In July Anna Akhmatova completed her poem "The Oath"; Konstantin Simonov, Polevoi and Vishnevsky sent their first dispatches from the battlefields; the artists N. Radlov, Yefimov and Kukryniks issued the first numbers of "TASS Display Windows" and performers of all the arts united in front-line concert teams.

At the Leningrad branch of the Composers' Union a "defense section" was actively at work, composing anti-Nazi songs for the masses. Already in July, their first songs—songs in placard, leaflet or lampoon form—were discussed at meetings of Union members, promptly mimeographed and distributed to recruitment offices and army hospitals, performed by visiting concert teams before front-line troops, and broadcast by radio. Among them was "An Oath to the Defense Commissar" by Shostakovich, which was soon commended as one of the best defense songs composed in the early months of the war.

Shostakovich was actively involved in the work of the defense section of the Composers' Union and the editorial board of the Leningrad subsidiary of the State Music Publishing House, which received a large heap of mail every day: songs, poems, etc.

In July 1941, Shostakovich joined the company of the Leningrad Theater of People's Volunteers directed by the actor Nikolai Cherkasov. They gave guest performances for front-line units, at military hospitals and at recruitment stations. As part of his daily duties, Shostakovich was to prepare accompaniments and arrangements and to play the piano accompaniment for musical numbers.

The composer's working day also included a military drill (compulsory for all members of Leningrad's branch of the Composer's Union), work at construction sites of defense fortifications (together with the professors and students of the Conservatory), patrol duty in local air-defense units, and participation in a volunteer fire brigade.

The situation in the city was getting more dangerous with every passing day. The front line was steadily drawing nearer, and it was already clear that the Nazi forces were encircling the city. On July 18, 1941, food rationing was introduced in Leningrad, which was being flooded with refugees from the environs. The art collections of the Hermitage and the Russian Museum, Pavlovsk, Pushkin and Peterhof were being evacuated. In August the evacuation of artistic institutions was announced: the Kirov Opera and Ballet Theater moved to Perm, MALEGOT to Orenburg, the Academic Choir to Kirov. At the end of the month, the Conservatory withdrew to Tashkent and the Leningrad Philharmonic left for Novosibirsk on one of the last trains. Shostakovich remained in the city as chairman of the Leningrad branch of the Composer's Union.

Shostakovich's burden of cares and duties as chairman had

grown enormously. But even after a full day's work, which claimed his unflagging attention, he invariably hastened to his home at No. 59 Bolshaya Pushkarskaya Street (house No. 37 today) to continue his work on the unfinished manuscript of his new composition—the Seventh Symphony. He worked very fast, seeking to express what lived in the hearts of the people and in his own heart via the language of music in the terse and solemn words of the military oath of allegiance.

On September 3, Shostakovich completed the first movement of the symphony, and on September 8 the Nazi pincers closed around Leningrad. Schlisselburg fell to the Nazis on the same day, and their air force and artillery unleashed their firepower on the city. In the evening the Badayev warehouse caught fire. A thick, black cloud of smoke from burning oil, butter, flour, sugar and groats hung over the city. The restless clicks of a metronome, broadcast over street loudspeakers, counted off the first minutes of the blockade. Life in the city, however, was going on. On the same day, September 8, the defense section held a regular meeting at the Leningrad branch of the Composer's Union, and the Musical Comedy Theater staged *The Bat*.

"Air alert! Three air alerts! Five air alerts! The siren has been whining all day . . ."
Entry in V. Inber's diary, September 14, 1941.

Toward mid-September, Nazi air strikes had become particularly fierce. It was a mild autumn, and the skies were cloudless and crystal clear, so air raids were almost incessant. The city was being shaken by explosions and the rumble of collapsing buildings, and its inhabitants were in the acrid smoke of the fires. On September 14, a mass meeting of young people was held. In the evening, Shostakovich played in a concert from which all box-office returns went to the national defense fund. Two days later, he completed the second movement of his symphony.

"My dear friends,

"I am speaking from Leningrad while fierce fighting is going on at its gates. I am speaking from a front-line city.

"Yesterday morning I completed the score of the second movement of my new, large symphony. If I succeed in my efforts to make a good composition and complete the third and fourth movements, it may be called the Seventh Symphony . . . I am telling this to make it known to all that the danger threatening Leningrad has not interrupted its full-blooded life."
Dmitry Shostakovich, "Leningrad, My Native City," *Sovietskoye Iskusstvo (Soviet Art),* September 18, 1941.

Even in the grim days of war, there was a time for simple joys: in their Moscow apartment, the Shostakoviches and their children are decorating a New Year tree. . .

An Epic Song

In October of 1942 Leonid Nikolayev died in Tashkent. Shostakovich wrote the mournful Second Piano Sonata, a requiem dedicated to his teacher's memory. The piano was the instrument that had linked them so intimately. The pupil paid his last respects to the teacher in the heartfelt music of the finale composed as a theme and variations. It had been Nikolayev's favorite form.

The war was in its second, and hardest, year. Its daily horrors literally rent Shostakovich's heart. Its every hour was a heavy blow which embittered his soul. Tragic news of friends and relatives, colleagues and pupils killed in action were coming from the war front. His simple emotions, so unprotected, now longed for expression.

He came upon a little volume of English and Scottish lyrical poetry. Its terse, unsophisticated lines exhaled the aroma of good old England, lute music, the simple charm of bagpipes and the rhythms of Scottish marches. Shostakovich composed his Six Romances based on poems by Sir Walter Raleigh, Robert Burns and William Shakespeare. The quiet and trustful intonations of the human voice: indeed, what musical instrument can be as sensitive, intimate and lively?

Shostakovich's six vocal miniatures called to life a simple and sincere world pervaded with the freedom-loving spirit of the old ballads of Robin Hood and his free forest fraternity, modest and unpretentious lyricism, the philosophic reflection of a sage, and the playful humor of a child. These scenes seemed far removed from modern reality and were a lyrical intermezzo of their own kind. The implication of the romances, however, was profound and meaningful, revealing the many-sided and majestic image of man aspiring toward justice and love at all times and courageously fighting evil.

In the autumn of 1943, when he had already moved to Moscow, Shostakovich resumed teaching at the Moscow Conservatory at the request of its director, Vissarion Shebalin. Simultaneously, he stepped up his activities as a performing musician. He played especially often at the Central Art Workers' Club, which was a permanent, perhaps the only, meeting place for members of the artistic community in war time.

He travelled from his home on the Mozhaiskoye Highway, to the city's central quarter almost daily during that autumn. In addition to his lessons at the Conservatory and performances in various concert halls around town, he was involved in public activities at the Organizing Committee of the Soviet Composers' Union. Moreover, he was obliged to attend rehearsals of his Eighth Symphony in the Grand Hall of the Moscow Conservatory started by the U.S.S.R. State Symphony Orchestra under the baton of Eugene Mravinsky.

"The dress rehearsal of Shostakovich's Eighth Symphony was to be held on the third [November]. As he entered the foyer, he exchanged greetings with many people he knew. Then he briskly came up to me and firmly shook my hand—firmly but with an absent look on his face. I could not read his mind, and I always wondered whether he was excited or calm. His boyish looks were the same: a taciturn frowning and embarrassed boy. He is extremely charismatic. He reminds me of a Martian as I imagined the Martians in my childhood. I can say nothing about the symphony at once, but I feel it is a composition of enormous power . . ."

Entry in V. Gusev's diary, November 8, 1943.

He had composed the symphony in the summer, staying at the Composers' Retreat at Ivanovo for the first time since the outbreak of the war. The large stone mansion, built at one time for a local squire, stood on the bank of a merrily gurgling stream winding its way towards the hazy strip of a distant forest where it vanished. In time the mansion passed into the possession of a large local state farm and later was handed over to the Composer's Union as a gift from the Soviet government. Tiny cottages, each for one family, sprang up around it. Musical instruments were available in the rooms, and additional lodges for composers were reserved in a neighboring village. The Ivanovo retreat offered cozy accommodations, not without a modicum of comfort, as its guests would recall after the war.

All residents of the Composers' Retreat were invariably busily at work: Prokofiev, Gliere, Shaporin, Muradeli, Kabalevsky and Shostakovich. The tension of wartime was felt constantly. In the quiet of that corner, though, far away from the theaters of war, the plain beauty of the Russian scenery looked especially majestic, and thoughts of the continuing war were agonizingly painful.

It had taken Shostakovich 40 days to write the Eighth Symphony to tell mankind of the terrible tragedy of war once again. One can guess from surviving manuscripts how fast the composer's hand darted over the sheets, how impatiently it crossed out discarded lines, how nervously drafts were torn up, and what painful efforts it took to bring forth the central musical ideas of the symphony.

Shostakovich listened to and assessed modern reality "from the inside," showed the world as it was seen and sensed by a human being caught up in a chaos of thundering metal and fire. It was not a chronicle or a panorama of events but a scene of the spiritual life of a people experiencing the tragedy of war.

Just as in the Fourth Symphony, the lyrical tragic substratum of Shostakovich's music was brought out with striking clarity. He is romantically frank and unrestrained, expressive and spontaneous in all manifestations of his artistic spirit. And again he asserts his right to portray a tragedy where optimism is born of collisions and struggle, where man is impelled to action by his maturity, courage and willpower.

"During the war I composed two symphonies and a number of chamber pieces. I wished to portray in musical imagery the spiritual life of a human being stunned by the gigantic hammer of war. I often linked his individual fate with the destinies of the masses, and they marched on together seized with fury, pain or jubilation ... This individual advances toward victory through tormenting trials and catastrophes. Now and then he falls to the ground, but he rises to his feet again ... His path is not strewn with roses nor is he accompanied by merry drummers."

Dmitry Shostakovich, *Our Wartime Work,* 1946.

All five movements of the symphony are devoted to the suffering and struggle of man at a gruelling time of trials. One has to pass through the first movement with its fierce shouts, struggle and pain, through the horrors of a "psychological" marching attack in the second and third movements, to survive an encounter with death, to sing a requiem for the dead in the fourth movement, to pass again through many stages of the violent struggle in the finale to see at last in its coda an unsteady and faint light—a gleam of hope, of love and of victory.

"This music astounds and amazes you; it wins you with a single word uttered in a whisper; it plunges you into a sea of dreams. Peals of thunder are interrupted by dances of the dead and songs of the living; a rest at the edge of a volcano; words of affection; the rumble of tanks; dreams of a happy life; the whiz of shells. Eventually, it will be a song of affection and a happy life that will have the final say.

"There is sensible optimism in this music. It is optimism of the year 1943. It is optimism worthy of the Soviet man of 1943. Thus the composition reveals itself in its finale, as was dictated by Aristotle, in a catharsis purifying the emotions through the effect of art."

Literatura i Iskusstvo (Literature and the Arts), November 7, 1943.

The symphony was first performed under Mravinsky's direction in Moscow on November 4, 1943. Critics were not unanimous in their assessment of it. Some of them deplored the absence of majestic brilliance in the finale and detested what they termed as cultivation of the images of evil and suffering. The composer was even accused of a certain degree of psychological instability. Time, however, would put everything in its right place. The Eighth Symphony would be recognized as one of the world's greatest art monuments to the Soviet people's courage in the Second World War.

Shortly before the war, Shostakovich plays his Piano Quintet with the Glazunov Quartet.

Above and opposite, lower photo:
"During the Great Patriotic War our writers, artists, and musicians are working hard and prolifically, because they are inspired by the most progressive ideas of our age. And as the cannons roar, our muses also raise their mighty heads. No one shall ever wrench the pen from our hands."

"During this time, I worked on my Seventh Symphony. I worked quickly and intensively. I wanted to compose a piece about today, about our life and our heroic people, fighting and conquering the enemy. Working on the symphony, I thought about the greatness and heroism of our nation, about mankind's greatest ideals. . . It is in the name of all this that we are fighting this cruel war. . . .I dedicate my Seventh Symphony to our struggle against fascism, to our coming victory, and to my native Leningrad."

On February 5 and 6, 1944, the Eighth Symphony was performed in Novosibirsk for the first time. Both concerts were introduced by Sollertinsky, who conveyed to the audience in his vivid and pictorial language his profound understanding of the dramaturgy and theme of the new composition. That was the last public address of the brilliant Soviet musicologist and critic. On the night of February 10 he died.

> "Dear Isaac,
>
> "I deeply grieve with you upon the loss of our near and dear friend Ivan Sollertinsky. I have no words to express the grief tormenting my heart. Let us keep his memory alive in our love for him and our faith in his brilliant talent and in his phenomenal devotion to the art for which he gave all of his beautiful life—the art of music. Sollertinsky is no more. This will be very hard to endure . . ."
>
> Excerpts from a letter by Dmitry Shostakovich to Isaac Glickmann, February 13, 1944.

A few days later, Shostakovich started to write his Trio for Violin, Cello and Piano in memory of Sollertinsky, strained and impassioned music full of sorrow and tragic thoughts. The Trio was first performed in Leningrad, where they had met and become friends way back in 1926 and where they had lived most of their lives.

After a few days the composer's new work was described in the newspaper *Leningradskaya Pravda*, and before long news of Shostakovich's Seventh Symphony spread throughout the world. Not yet completed or performed in public, the symphony became a symbol of the courage and staunchness of besieged Leningrad, a symbol of the heroic struggle waged by the whole country. Already in the autumn of 1941 the best American conductors —Eugene Ormandy, Leopold Stokowski, Serge Koussevitzky and Arturo Toscanini, among others—showered the Soviet embassy with letters requesting the right to the first performance of the symphony in the United States.

> "The Nazis have taken Kiev . . . I was excited to learn that even in these days Shostakovich is writing a symphony in the besieged city [Leningrad] bombed and shelled by the enemy. What is most important, *Leningradskaya Pravda* reported this fact along with dispatches from the Southern front and stories about 'Nazi vultures' and 'Molotov cocktails.' This means that art has not died, that it is alive, shining and warming the heart. Apollo has not yet been strangled by Mars."
>
> Entry in V. Inber's diary, September 22, 1941.

Shostakovich still continued his work at the Composers' Union and in the publishing house, and at certain hours served on patrol duty as a rank-and-file member of an air defense unit. He also gave instruction to a few Conservatory students who had remained in the city, performed in concerts arranged to contribute to the defense fund, played at the Theater of People's Volunteers and made two visits to the front line. Nevertheless, on September 29 he completed the third movement of the symphony: the broad and majestic adagio. "I have never composed so quickly as now," he said at the time.

Twelve days of war time to compose music about peace! Days planned to the minute, days of incessant fierce Nazi air raids. All his physical strength and creative talent were strained to the limit, but his confidence in ultimate victory never faltered. That was how Shostakovich worked together with all Leningraders and the country as a whole.

"On September 28, 1941, . . . Tchaikovsky's Fifth Symphony was on the program . . . On that day an air alert was announced 11 times. Shortly before the concert began, a bomb had hit house No. 4 on Proletcult Street near the offices of the Leningrad Broadcasting Studios. One wing was damaged, and all windows were shattered, of course. Studio personnel were immediately sent to clear the debris, but the concert began exactly as scheduled. The first two movements of the symphony were played without obstruction. At the beginning of the third movement, there was a fierce air raid. The performance went on to the incessant accompaniment of barking ack-ack fire shaking the studio walls. The last strains of the Fifth Symphony had died down, but the all clear was not yet announced. The members of the orchestra who were attached to air-defense units went to their duty stations."

Karl Eliasberg, *The Leningrad Broadcasting Studios in the Great Patriotic War,* 1946.

Early in October, Shostakovich flew to Moscow at the request of the Military Commissariat. Barrage balloons were lazily floating over the capital's airport, and the first thing he heard when leaving the plane was the ringing voices of an anti-aircraft gun crew. The front line had broken through at Smolensk, the Nazis were approaching Kalinin, and the last rings of defense fortifications were closing in the city. Life in the city, however, went on as usual. On October 11 a group of Moscow musicians assembled at the offices of the newspapers *Sovietskoye Iskusstvo (Soviet Art)* to acquaint themselves with the three movements of Shostakovich's new symphony.

". . . The Seventh Symphony will be the most dramatic one among Shostakovich's latest compositions. His voice has grown stronger; the lyricism of philosophic meditation has given way to civic sentiments; the subjective has been replaced by the objective common to all humanity; the theme of the individual hero has been ousted by thoughts of the destiny of the country and people . . . The symphony has no finale yet, but it can be guessed in its three movements already composed; it is the image of victory built up by the inner logic of the music, of triumph over the dark forces of fascism."

Sovietskoye Iskusstvo (Soviet Art), October 16, 1941.

The finale of the symphony was written in Kuibyshev in December 1941. The Bolshoi orchestra stayed here after its evacuation from Moscow. Its art director and chief conductor, Samuel Samosud, was the first to take the clean copy of the score of Shostakovich's new composition.

Originally, the composer had planned to prefix all movements of the symphony with brief program titles: "The War," "Reminiscences," "The Native Land" and "Victory." Soon, however, he removed them, realizing perhaps the imperfections of verbal descriptions.

> "I wanted to write a composition about our times, our life, and our people who become heroes, who fight in the name of our triumph over the enemy, who perform feats of valor and win."
>
> Dmitry Shostakovich, "The Seventh Symphony," *Pravda*, March 29, 1942.

There is hardly another musical composition of the 20th century which attracted as much attention and interest as Shostakovich's Seventh (Leningrad) Symphony. It became a veritable document of Soviet history and evoked an unprecedented public response throughout the world. The concepts of patriotism, courage, heroism, struggle and victory—all these were concentrated in the Leningrad Symphony. Few musical compositions had given rise to such a vast number of articles, reviews and pamphlets.

The music of the first movement, which was to absorb all the thematic material of the symphony, as the composer had tentatively planned, has an enormous force of expression. Its main themes are salient and concrete in the extreme. There are the calm and majestic theme of the motherland, which asserts itself with dignity, and the exaggeratedly mechanistic theme of the invasion. The sibilant endings of musical phrases are reminiscent of either a pompous Nazi march or a cheap beer-hall tune, which were circulated by the hundreds through the cities and streets of the Third Reich, intoxicated with its "victories." On the one hand, there are the epic power and full-blooded orchestral sound of the warm timbres of the strings and the manly voices of the brass, and the broad, unconstrained breathing of phrases, a clear reliance on song intonations. On the other hand, there is an unnatural, ghastly combination of the piccolo flute and the small drum, the heartless automatism of an endlessly repeated short, rhythmic phrase imitating the roll of an army drum. The events of the tragedy unfolding before the listener are monstrous. Equally monstrous and terrible is the force which suddenly grows out of what seems to be an almost innocent tavern song in the famous invasion episode. Through the medium of music alone, a citizen and artist of Russia speaks of fascism with anger and pain. This is followed by a quiet monologue by the bassoon.

The second movement is a misty elegiac scene of the country's peaceful past; the third is calm reflection, full of lofty feeling; the finale revives—through struggle, suffering and death—the initial theme of the first movement, the theme of the motherland, and in the final strains of the symphony it predicts the victory which is to come.

Shostakovich was the first Soviet composer to respond to modern developments in a genre which had for centuries required a distance in time for philosophical comprehension. Precisely, a symphony was a composition of superlative historical veracity and artistic generalization. The music of the Seventh Symphony is remarkable for its powerful force, broad scope, great passion and superior mastery.

The premiere of the Seventh Symphony was held in Kuibyshev on March 5, 1942. The Bolshoi orchestra under the baton of Samosud had prepared its performance in record time. *Pravda's* war correspondent Alexei Tolstoy, who had attended rehearsals, sent a delighted article to his newspaper, which read like a battle report.

> "The Seventh Symphony has arisen from the conscience of the Russian people who without hesitation gave battle to the dark forces of fascism. Written in Leningrad, it has grown to the magnitude of great art understandable to people in all parts of the world because it tells the truth about man at a time of unprecedented suffering and trials. The symphony is transparent despite its enormous complexity; it is stern and lyrically virile and all of it is in flight towards the future lying beyond man's victory over the Nazi beast. The Red Army has created a formidable symphony of worldwide victory; Shostakovich has lent his ear to the throbbing heart of the Motherland and played a song of triumph."

Alexei Tolstoy, *Pravda*, February 16, 1942.

Following the triumphant success of the premiere in Kuibyshev, the symphony was performed in Moscow on March 29. On June 1, a plane carrying its score on microfilm landed in New York. On June 22, 1942, exaclty one year after Nazi Germany's attack on the Soviet Union, the symphony was performed under the baton of Henry Wood in London and its New York premiere under the direction of Toscanini was slated for July 19.

The orchestra of the Leningrad Philharmonic, which had been evacuated to Novosibirsk, was also rehearsing for the first performance of the symphony. The score, brought by air, was copied out in parts in a matter of days. Rehearsals were started and after Shostakovich's arrival they became more intensive and inspired. The premiere was fixed for July 9.

> "I am happy to know that the musicians of this first-class orchestra are now rehearsing my Seventh Symphony. Already the first few rehearsals carried out by the orchestra and conductor with exceptional creative inspiration have shown that my symphony will be performed excellently. I am looking forward to the premiere with great impatience."

Dmitry Shostakovich, "The Premiere of the Seventh Symphony," *Sovietskaya Sibir (Soviet Siberia)*, July 4, 1942.

Premieres of the symphony also took place in Erevan and Tashkent. A hall in Tashkent, in far away Central Asia, was packed with professors and students of the Leningrad Conservatory evacuated there. There was a standing ovation.

In Leningrad the premiere was set for August 9, 1942, the date which the Nazis had chosen for entering the city. Its score in four voluminous hardcover copybooks had been flown to Leningrad as far back as May, but it had seemed at first that the symphony could not be performed there, since less than half of the orchestra members required by the score were available. But now the city, which was the hero of the symphony, was assisted by army bands who sent their best musicians to work under the direction of Karl Eliasberg. Each rehearsal was an unprecedented exploit of the musicians emaciated by hunger and fatigue, but their enthusiasm was as infinite as the courage of those who would fill the hall of the Leningrad Conservatory on August 9.

> ". . . People would come to listen to his music. They would slowly but stubbornly move through the city, struggling alone on their swollen feet and supporting one another . . . They would often stop to take a rest, and for many the path to his music would last for hours. But come they would. They would come to borrow from the Seventh Symphony a new lease on life and unfailing faith in their ultimate victory over the forces of evil."
>
> Leo Arnstam, *The Music of the Heroic*, 1977.

In 1942 Shostakovich was awarded a U.S.S.R. State Prize and the title of Merited Art Worker of the Russian Federation for his Seventh Symphony, and in 1943 the American Academy of Arts and Letters elected him to honorary membership. That was the beginning of his worldwide recognition and fame.

The Symphony for the End of the War

Shostakovich's wartime activities as a performing musician were closely tied to Radio Moscow. Here he played solo parts or in concert, particularly often with the Beethoven Quartet. Recordings were made in the studios at night. Sometimes three or four programs at a time had to be prepared. Old-timers of Radio Moscow still remember him as a calm and cheerful man who never looked tired, despondent or indifferent. When his musician colleagues were utterly exhausted, he cracked jokes and tactfully encouraged them, and they carried on their work with renewed energy. Shortly after the war, in 1946, Shostakovich would write his Third Quartet, full of anguished thoughts about the tragedy just experienced, and dedicate it to the Beethoven Quartet in memory of their joint work in the war years.

Programs of Russian and Soviet classics were prepared for foreign listeners. His Quintet was also played. That was symbolic. Music in which quiet, tranquility and spiritual harmony reigned supreme came on the air filled with the anxious and stern voices of war and confidently blazed the trail to mankind's most radiant hopes and dreams. It spoke of the Soviet people's courage, heroism and indomitable will.

After the lifting of the siege of Leningrad, Shostakovich came back to his native city to play in the Grand Hall of the Leningrad Philharmonic as before. One of the first compositions he played in concert with D. Tsiganov and S. Shirinsky of the Beethoven Quartet was the Trio in Memory of Sollertinsky. As soon as Tsiganov entered the dressing room during an intermission, Shostakovich burst in. There were tears in his eyes. "I've seen many people in their customary seats!" he exclaimed. The wonderful tradition of Leningrad music lovers to have their permanent seats in the Philharmonic hall was still alive. That was an expression of the staunch spirit of the city's defenders and a recognition of the eternal value of the world of art.

The war was drawing to a close. That could be guessed from the happy faces of people arriving in the city and those who met them at the railway stations, from the exhaustive work being done in towns to improve their general appearance, from the proud intonations of radio announcers reading *Sovinformbureau* communiqués, from the thunder of gun salutes in honor of new victories for the Soviet Union.

Shostakovich got down to work on his Ninth Symphony. It was rumored within music circles that this would be a large composition with a chorus and soloists. All expected a magnificent eulogy praising the courage and heroism of the Soviet people. Such a composition was to crown Shostakovich's trilogy of wartime symphonies: the Leningrad Symphony, a poignant chronicle of war; the Eighth Symphony, a mournful song of suffering; the Ninth Symphony, the triumph of victory.

Many Soviet composers were engaged in quests of new heroic music. They were looking for fresh majestic intonations to convey the spirit of martial music and for special orchestral facilities using bells, blazing trumpets, and impressive percussions. They also turned to compositions conforming to the character of this music: cantata, symphony, overture, ode, and vocal-symphonic poem. Vano Muradeli dedicated his Second Symphony "to the Soviet people's victory over fascism." Sergei Prokofiev was planning to compose an "Ode to the End of the War" for eight harps, four pianos, an orchestra of wind and percussion instruments and double basses.

Shostakovich had begun his work on the Ninth Symphony in the winter of 1944-45. However, his composition of a solemn heroic canvas proceeded slowly and laboriously, and he was haunted by doubts. It was in August that he quickly completed it after changing its conception, which gave him a growing sense of self-assurance.

"The Ninth Symphony differs strikingly in character

from my earlier symphonies, the Seventh and the Eighth. Both the latter were tragic-heroic, while in the Ninth a transparent, clear and light mood prevails. The symphony consists of five small movements . . ."

Dmitry Shostakovich. Excerpt from a *Sovietskoye Iskusstvo (Soviet Art)* interview, September 7, 1945.

The musical public was puzzled. Intended for the triumphal consummation of the trilogy, the symphony seemed to be completely at variance with its lofty purpose. Not only was it unusually short (its five movements lasted only 22 minutes!) but its content, in the opinion of many, was unusually shallow. So its premiere held in Leningrad by the Leningrad Philharmonic Orchestra under Eugene Mravinsky's direction did not evoke unanimous admiration. Its assessments by music critics revealed their skepticism and disappointment.

A familiar situation, was it not? A few years earlier, the light and graceful Sixth Symphony had been received just as skeptically. It looked well nigh sacrilegious after the tragic confession of the Fourth (which was known to many) and the impassioned drama of the Fifth. The wartime trilogy described the same paradoxical circle in a new spiral, a new stage in the evolution of Shostakovich's art. The crown of the trilogy was a symphony scherzo again. And it would again take time for Shostakovich's wisdom and integrity as an artist to become apparent to everyone.

The Ninth Symphony was a direct and obvious offspring of victory. Victory alone could have called to life this merry, festive and ironic composition. It charms one with the perfection and precision of its language, its amazing, almost childlike frankness and openheartedness. It is not accidental that it echoes the music of the Viennese classics—of Haydn, Mozart and even Rossini—and the juvenile compositions of Shostakovich himself—the music of films, ballets and dramas.

For all its lightness, however, the Ninth Symphony is not shallow. This quality was absolutely alien to the composer-philosopher. Its fourth movement—the funeral procession and the mournful oration over the grave of the fallen victims—is profoundly moving. The sinister image of a convulsively wriggling puppet flashes at times amid general jubilation in the finale as well. Nevertheless, the symphony scherzo, illuminated with the lights of holiday salutes and filled with the noise of a holiday crowd, is the most classical and perfectly transparent composition in Shostakovich's music. This music consummates his great wartime trilogy. With this music, his Symphony for the End of the War has gone down in history.

A Great Citizen

Turning the Tide

The Soviet government bestowed lavish honors on those who had won victory in World War II in recognition of their courage and determination. Many were decorated posthumously. As far back as 1943, Shostakovich had been awarded a medal "for the defense of Leningrad," and in 1946, when the 80th anniversary of the Moscow Conservatory was celebrated, Professor Shostakovich was decorated with the Order of Lenin for his signal contributions to the progress of Soviet music. A little later, he won a U.S.S.R. State Prize for his Trio in Memory of Sollertinsky.

The year 1946 was a time for rebuilding the country. In March a new Five-Year-Plan for economic recovery and development was adopted, and the country vigorously set to work on its top-priority tasks. In the Donets Basin, war-ravaged coal mines went back into production one after another, the mighty arch of the Dnieper power dam was rebuilt rapidly, and the first postwar batch of tractors rolled off the conveyor belt of the Kharkov Tractor Works.

Soviet art was also grappling with tasks of fundamental importance. In October 1946, the Organizing Committee of the Soviet Composers' Union held plenary meeting in Moscow. It was the first widely representative musical form to discuss ways of further developing Soviet music to be held in postwar Russia.

It seemed to many theoreticians of art and to the artists themselves that the people who had experienced the hardships of the most terrible war in mankind's history would hardly welcome compositions on a philosophically tragic, or say, sharply satirical plane. This viewpoint oriented writers, painters, musicians and art directors to producing works mainly in a solemn, but buoyant key. Debates became heated, and opinions differed as widely as ever.

At that stage in the development of Soviet music, the Feburary 10, 1948, resolution of the Central Committee of the Soviet Communist Party "On the Opera *Great Friendship* by V. Muradeli" was important. It clearly outlined Party policy in the field of culture and proposed practical measures to "ensure the development of Soviet music in a realistic direction." A number of composers were sternly reproached for their "disregard for the demands and artistic taste of the Soviet people." Shostakovich was mentioned among others, and his opera *Lady Macbeth of Mtsensk* and his Fourth, Sixth, Eighth and Ninth symphonies were denounced as formalistic works.

Shostakovich with the great German writer and anti-war activist Bertolt Brecht in Berlin.

Opposite:
Shostakovich and his friend Isaac Glickmann in the country near Leningrad.

The atmosphere of tension around Shostakovich's compositions was not dispelled until a few years later. In 1958 the CPU [Communist Party of the Soviet Union] Central Committee pointed out that the Resolution of 1948, which had "set correct guidelines for developing Soviet art on the principles of kinship with folk art and realism and which justly criticized some misguided, formalistic trends in music, contained a few unfair and unjustifiably severe criticisms of the art of some talented composers." All that time, Shostakovich had been constantly at work, asserting the justice of his own position in art.

> "Not infrequently, 'formalism' is a label applied to what is not quite comprehensible or even unpalatable to some persons . . . However, only art which is empty and devoid of ideas, cold and lifeless, deserves to be described as a formalistic art. In the latter, the technique chosen by the composer becomes an end in itself, a kind of foppery, a trick of an aesthete."
>
> Dmitry Shostakovich, "Some Pressing Problems of Musical Art," *Pravda*, June 17, 1956.

Searches for new themes, a constant striving for breathing new life into his compositions through lexical means, conditioned the specific orientation of Shostakovich's artistic ambitions in the late 1940's and early '50s. Over a period of eight years, he added to the list of his compositions two cantatas, an oratorio, two quartets, a violin concerto, and a host of vocal chamber pieces and film opuses. The composer again felt the need to reflect on his record in retrospect and to explore new and untrodden ground. It was not fortuitous that he wrote so much vocal music and incidental music for films in these years. His interest in new themes and new forms held out the promise of new successes and new revelations.

In 1948, he completed his vocal cycle *From Jewish Folk Poetry*. Its 11 genre scenes are literally pervaded with music of everyday life and call to mind Alexander Dargomyzhsky's *Titular Counselor* and Modest Moussorgsky's *Callistratus* and *Nursery*. This cycle is remarkably reminiscent of its great classical predecessors in that its everyday life intonations and genres were for the first time interpreted by the composer not as an object for a parody but seriously, with full sympathy, kindness and respect. Indeed, how else could a humanist composer have interpreted the theme of a humble human being without rights, a hero new to him but eternal to art?

In 1949 Shostakovich began his public activities in the antiwar movement. As a member of the Soviet Peace Committee, he went to the United States with a representative Soviet delegation to attend the Cultural and Scientific Conference for World Peace to be held in New York City. He delivered a report to a meeting at the department of music, poetry, painting and choreography. As it was his first visit to such a responsible international forum, Shostakovich sensed especially keenly his involvement in the most vital issues of modern life.

"The part we play in society as artists and musicians, as members of the artistic intelligentsia, is exceedingly great. We must forcefully raise our voices for peace, for truth, for humaneness, for the future of nations. At these decisive stages of history, we must not withdraw from reality and nurture the silly illusion of existence on a higher plane than real life and struggle. We must enter the very midst of life to be able to influence its course. We must march in step with mankind's progressive forces in the front ranks of peace fighters. We must take part in this struggle through our art, its content, ideas, images and aims. We must add the beautiful and powerful voice of our art to the courageous voices of the people. . . ."

Dmitry Shostakovich. Excerpt from a speech at the Cultural and Scientific Conference for World Peace in the United States, March 30, 1949.

In 1950 Shostakovich attended the Second U.S.S.R. Peace Conference and then went to the Second World Peace Congress in Warsaw. In 1951 he delivered a speech at the Third U.S.S.R. Peace Conference. In 1952 he spoke at the fourth such conference and was elected to the Soviet Peace Committee. His outstanding services to the cause of peace won him the 1954 International Peace Prize of the World Peace Council.

In 1950 the Bach Music Festival was held in Leipzig to commemorate the bicentenary of the death of the great German composer. The large Soviet delegation consisted of music critics, composers and performers. Dmitry Shostakovich came as a guest and a member of the jury of the Bach International Contest. He also gave a piano recital—a fairly rare occurrence now—of Bach's Concerto for Three Claviers and Orchestra, in concert with Tatiana Nikolayeva and Pavel Serebryakov, on the final day of the contest.

The profound philosophical message of Bach's music was received in a new way at the festival. The resounding vaults of St. Thomas's Church preserved the spirit of old Protestant Germany, the spirit of petty burghers and religious humility, as well as the spirit of lofty art and solemn organ music. Upon his return to Moscow, Shostakovich wrote a cycle of 24 preludes and fugues for piano, which amazes the listener with its filigree polyphony and its rich gamut of emotions.

As had often happened after stormy periods and social cataclysms in earlier history, the postwar years witnessed an enormous growth of interest in the themes and images of art of the past. Modern art was seeking in its classical heritage a fulcrum on which to rely in resisting the tragic discord of the present world. The dramatic feeling of the ancient myths, the lofty philosophic message of baroque music, the moral imperatives of the classical theater, the eternal themes of life and death, good and evil, love and duty, were indispensable for comprehending the problems of the 20th century.

The devoted father with his daughter Galina, in 1948.

Shostakovich and director Grigory Kosintzev (right) collaborated on many films, including such masterpieces as *Hamlet* and *King Lear*. ". . .I feel I can look upon myself as one of the pioneers in the field of film music. . . .Cinema work opens up vast possibilities for the composer and can be of invaluable benefit to him."

Shostakovich and his colleague Tikhon Khrennikov greet a distinguished guest—composer Benjamin Britten, whom Shostakovich considered "one of the most talented among foreign composers" and to whom he dedicated his Fourteenth Symphony.

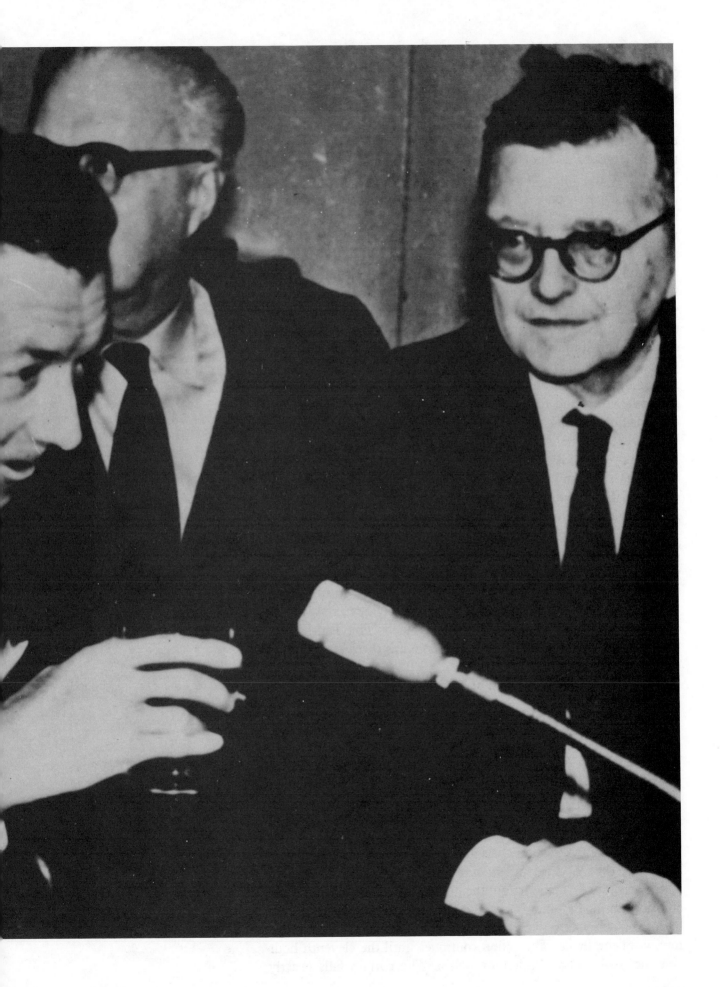

On October 10, 1951, the Academic Russian Choir directed by A. Sveshnikov introduced Moscow's music lovers to Shostakovich's new composition: Ten Poems by Revolutionary Poets for Mixed Chorus. The composer was trying his hand at another unfamiliar genre: the choral song *a cappella*. This was destined to become the threshold beyond which lay a straight road toward large-scale symphonic and vocal-symphonic canvases of the late 1950s and early '60s on themes from Russian history.

He had chosen poets molded by the revolutionary labor movement in Russia and turned to choral polyphony, whose sounds resurrected the atmosphere of May Day protests and clandestine meetings. He had borrowed the intonations of revolutionary songs, not for direct quotation, but for introducing a measure of faithfulness that would allow a rich gamut of associations to be perceived in the music of the poems. He had revived the traditions of Russian classical opera, preeminent in Moussorgsky's epic dramas, with its profound revelation of the spirit and fate of the people. Finally, he had again displayed the romantic side of his artistic nature by choosing the musical language of poetry to narrate his country's proud history. The country highly appreciated this composition of one of its finest artists. He was awarded the U.S.S.R. State Prize for 1952.

After a year, Shostakovich completed his Tenth Symphony. The eight years which had elapsed since the Ninth had noticeably changed the composer's symphonic handwriting. The colors of harmony and orchestration had become softer, and the melodies now clearly traceable to Russian folk songs had become even more lyrical and expressive. Shostakovich seemed to be testing the dependability of the symphonic structure loaded with novel melodic material that would make the basis for his future plans. Significantly, this music, which sounded largely new, resolved an earlier theme painfully crucial to Shostakovich. The Tenth Symphony is just as tragic and full of confession as the finest pages of the Fourth or Eighth symphonies.

> "One need not be afraid of bold, creative quests but of 'comfortable' gliding over the surface, of drabness and monotony. I believe that a desire to iron out sharp angles in art is a peculiar manifestation of the 'theory of non-conflictiveness.' The sooner we discard these levelling tendencies the better it will be for the progress of Soviet art."
>
> Dmitry Shostakovich, "The Joy of Creative Quests," *Sovietskaya Muzyka* (Soviet Music), No. 1, 1954.

The limits of the classical cycle in four movements impose no constraints on the free development of musical thought passing through all the stages of dramatic action: the heat and acuity of psychological collisions in the first movement, the sinister battle scenes in the second, the gloomy narrative in the third, and the dynamic and restless motion of the finale. The action continues until the eleventh hour and the final message is left unspoken. The curtain falls exactly when the "hero" slowly moves towards the floodlights.

In the Tenth Symphony, Shostakovich raised the problem of the finale for a public discussion for the tenth time. He again broached this subject, which could not be ignored any longer, in his music and his article "The Joy of Creative Quests." That was a time when the problem of the finale—a cheerful and happy one, as a rule—seemed to be nonexistent. It was precisely the finale that gave rise to a bitter controversy over the principles of symphonic composition, in which divergent opinions were expressed about Shostakovich's Tenth Symphony and Soviet symphonic music in general, with an intransigence and vehemency reminiscent of the early years of the Revolution.

> "Shostakovich could not have written a smooth symphony . . . Indeed, the Tenth Symphony is full of dramatic tension. This drama, however, is not one of hopelessness. This is an optimistic tragedy inspired with passionate faith in the eventual triumph of lucid, life-asserting forces."
>
> *Sovietskaya Muzyka (Soviet Music),* No. 3, 1954.

Events of the next period confirmed the validity of this view, and the heated and long-continued debates over the Tenth Symphony eventually gave a powerful stimulus to the creativity of Soviet symphonists. In 1954 Shostakovich had the title of People's Artist of the U.S.S.R. bestowed upon him, and on the occasion of his 50th birthday he was decorated with a second Order of Lenin.

A Heroic Chronicle

The war was a test of endurance which compelled many to take a new look at the country's revolutionary record. The revived feeling of national pride intensified a thousand-fold, just as in the early post-revolutionary years there was an interest in the past, particularly in the most complex epochs which radically changed the time-honored political, ideological and ethical criteria.

That interest did not suggest an idle or nostalgic admiration for old Russia's picturesque fair shows, dressed-up merchant's wives, tame bears and merry-go-rounds. It was rather a new look at Russian history in its periods of crucial, sometimes tragic, change and at Russian characters of famous in legend for the nobleness and universal moral appeal which put them above the rapid flow of time.

Shostakovich devoted the year 1957 to his work on the Eleventh Symphony, *1905*, which became the first chapter of his musical history of Russia. Resurrecting the events of the 1905 uprisings, the composer addressed the country as an impassioned orator and tribune in a tone that was unmistakably honest and convincing. He dreamed of recreating in music a majestic and austere, audible and visible, image of history, which spoke to him in the language of songs.

Shostakovich and his wife Nina, who
died in 1954.

In the course of his life, Shostakovich came into contact with many people who, like himself, had a part in shaping the musical scene of the times. *Above:* Shostakovich with world-famous conductor Herbert von Karajan and renowned Soviet musicologist Lev Ginsburg (right). *Below:* Shostakovich with two fellow composers, Sergei Prokofiev and Aram Khachaturian.

Shostakovich revived in the Eleventh Symphony the revolutionary song as a direct quotation, as a slogan, as an appeal to the memory of the people.

> "Who else but people of my generation or those who are slightly younger remember today the revolutionary songs our young workers and students loved so much half a century ago? Another half century will elapse, and they will pass into oblivion; they could not be forgotten, of course, if it were not for the genius of music which has absorbed and synthesized the voices of suffering, struggling and living mankind . . ."
>
> M. Shaginyan, *Shostakovich's Eleventh Symphony*, 1957.

The symphony contains quite a few revolutonary songs: "The Prisoner," "Listen, Comrade!" "The Warsaw March," "Rage, Tyrants!" and "March in Step, Friends!" They mingle and transform into one another and merge into a sea of melodies like banners merging into a sea of red at a workers' demonstration. The song so thoroughly pervades the fabric of the symphony that it breaks the traditional laws and rules of form construction. Its four movements ("Palace Square," "The 9th of January," "Eternal Memory," "The Tocsin") follow in succession as four sections of a large and powerful song about the country's history.

Shostakovich dedicated the Eleventh Symphony to the 40th anniversary of the October Revolution. It was first performed in Moscow on October 30, 1957, a week before the holiday, and in 1958 he was awarded the Lenin Prize for this composition.

> "The imaginative musical thinking, the pictorial means of expression, the clear-cut musical dramaturgy of the symphony, are so vivid that one listens to it as if it were an opera without a text. Following the finest traditions of the Russian classics, Moussorgsky first and foremost, and speaking from the level of symphonic philosophic generalization, Shostakovich narrates of the revolutionary events of 1905 . . . It is to be hoped that Shostakovich's symphony . . . will be a prologue to new compositions about the epoch of socialist revolution . . ."
>
> *Leningradskaya Pravda*, November 12, 1957.

The author of the review published in *Leningradskaya Pravda* was not disappointed: in three years' time, Shostakovich would begin work on the second chapter of his musical history. For the time being, he concerned himself with a different matter: in the spring and summer of 1958 he made a few visits abroad.

> "Composer Dmitry Shostakovich, People's Artist of the U.S.S.R., went to Italy on May 9 at the invitation of the Santa Cecilia Academy of Music."
>
> *Sovietskaya Kultura (Soviet Culture)*, May 10, 1958.

> "Paris. May 22 (TASS). The solemn ceremony of proclaiming the Soviet composer Dmitry Shostakovich a knight commander of the French Order of Arts and Letters was held here today."
>
> *Sovietskaya Kultura (Soviet Culture)*, May 23, 1958.

"On June 25, the title of Honorary Doctor of Music was conferred on Dmitry Shostakovich at a solemn ceremony at Oxford . . ."

Pravda, June 26, 1958.

Shostakovich's collection of honorary diplomas and titles from universities, musical societies, institutions and organizations rapidly grew: the Swedish Royal Academy of Music (1954), Italy's Santa Cecilia Academy (1956), Britain, France, Austria, Finland, Mexico, the United States, Serbia, Bavaria . . . In almost every country the honoring ceremony was accompanied by a performance of his compositions. That was the case, for instance, in France, where he was inducted as a knight commander into the Order of Arts and Letters. The ceremony was held on May 22, and on May 27 his Eleventh Symphony was first performed in the biggest concert hall, "Pleyel," of Paris.

Great Britain's oldest college, Oxford University, bestowed on Shostakovich the title of Honorary Doctor of Music at a ceremony attended by heads of colleges, eminent professors and scholars of the United Kingdom. There were long gowns reaching the floor, ancient headgear worn only on the most solemn occasions, stiff and high-flown Latin. An ancient English university was honoring a modern Soviet composer.

After some time, Shostakovich again surprised his colleagues and admirers by an unexpected change of subject. This man curiously combined a serious cast of mind and a sense of humor, concentration and lightheartedness. That was evident in his art as well. The Fourth and Fifth Symphonies were followed by the Sixth, the Eighth by the Ninth, but the Eleventh Symphony was followed by—an operetta.

Shostakovich was in a quiet and cheerful mood. Moscow was building fast, bettering its looks and putting on a green attire. Trucks carried furniture of every description to brand-new prefab neighborhoods in the southwest section of the city. There were the noise and laughter of house-warming parties, the fascination of new encounters, occasional misunderstandings quickly resolved, and the beginnings of long friendships. Why not write a mischievous musical comedy on this subject? Without much hesitation Shostakovich wrote it. It was named after the section of the city *Cheremushki, Moscow*.

"It's really good when a truly great composer turns to the merry genre of operetta, always topical and invariably favored by the public. It's good when he is a success, and the public gets a work that's gay and highly artistic at the same time. It's still better to have a work so interesting as to warrant a discussion on the nature and future of the very genre of operetta. Shostakovich's new composition is the right thing to have in this respect. The charm of the comedy emanates from the music, of course. Shostakovich has proved that he can accomplish anything without departing from his principles even

Shostakovich, composer Tikhon Khrennikov, and others, enjoying a sunny afternoon in a park.

A 1953 picture of Dmitry Shostakovich, inscribed "to dear Lev Solomonovich Ginsburg with the best of wishes."

Above: **A display of the foreign awards received by Dmitry Shostakovich.** *Below:* **The composer resting at his country house.**

Shostakovich in his study.

slightly . . . This operetta has absorbed a lot of folk melodies, both domestic and foreign, and all this music had undergone a wonderful transformation and received a new lease on life."

Literaturny Noviny (Literary News), Prague, February 1959.

In the summer of 1960, Shostakovich went to Dresden. He was to write the music for the film *Five Days, Five Nights* that Soviet cinematographers were making jointly with their colleagues in East Germany. He rambled through the streets of Dresden and recalled the streets of Leningrad ravaged by war and the siege.

"The Eighth Quartet was composed in three days in Dresden while the film *Five Days, Five Nights* was in production. It would seem it is impossible not only to compose but even to write down a piece of five parts for a chamber orchestra in such a short time. The film takes us back to the theme of the last war. The new string quartet Shostakovich wrote for the material filmed for the movie is dedicated to the memory of the victims of war and fascism . . ."

Izvestia, October 22, 1960.

His hand quickly ran across the paper on which he was writing down the music bursting out of his heart. He had never worked so fast except, perhaps, while he was composing the Seventh and Eighth symphonies. This lyrical epic presented the theme of the last war in a largely new light. The music of the Eighth Quartet entwined in its fabric intonations of the First Symphony, the Piano Trio, the song "Tortured to Death by Hard Labor," the opera *Lady Macbeth* and, what is most important, the sound monogram D, Es, C, H (D, E flat, C, B) forming Shostakovich's initials in the Cyrillic alphabet like the voice of the composer himself. This reference to himself had a profound meaning to the composer, who regarded his own life as inseparably bound up with the destiny of his country.

In the autumn of the same year, 1960, Shostakovich spoke over Radio Moscow and in the press about his new Twelfth Symphony. Just as many years ago when, as soon as he had completed two movements of his Seventh Symphony, he hastened to share his plans with his countrymen for whom he worked and created his impassioned music, now he addressed them again to describe his new work, so vital to him. The composer visualized his future audience as a multimillion contingent of like-minded comrades. Among them were heroes of his Seventh Symphony and of the future Twelfth Symphony. He wanted his new symphony to be understandable to the people and consonant with their sentiments, and he described his new conception willingly and in detail. He was to write the second chapter of the musical history of Russia.

"I am now working on my Twelfth Symphony. When I was completing my Eleventh Symphony, I began thinking of its continuation; that was how the conception of the Twelfth came into being ... Two of the four movements of the symphony are almost finished. The symphony will be dedicated simultaneously to the October Revolution and to the memory of Lenin. I have conceived its first movement as a musical story of Lenin's arrival in Petrograd in April 1917, and his meeting with the working people of Petrograd. The second movement will reflect the heroic events of November 7. The third movement will tell of the civil war, and the fourth movement of the victory of the Great October Socialist Revolution."

Dmitry Shostakovich. Excerpt from a Radio Moscow broadcast, October 29, 1960.

In the process of composition, the original conception was perfected, as was often the case in Shostakovich's work and he gave the symphony a slightly different program from his original plan. In the first movement ("Revolutionary Petrograd"), the city, gathering forces for an uprising, roars powerfully and formidably like an inexorably advancing avalanche. The second movement ("Razliv," named after Lenin's hideout during the summer of 1917) unhurried and philosophically concentrated, portrays the image of Lenin deciding the destiny of the country and revolution. In the third movement ("Aurora"), the thunder of the guns of the legendary cruiser *Aurora* shakes the old world to its foundations, announcing the "final and decisive battle." The fourth movement ("The Dawn of Humanity") is a majestic apotheosis exalting freedom, equality and happiness on earth.

This rhetoric and solemn music was reminiscent in some imperceptible way of the *Dedication to October* and the *May Day* Symphony. However, it was free from the naive straightforwardness of those early compositions. The composer had lived a long life and understood his time in all its greatness, without interference of trivia and workaday details. The Twelfth Symphony was an epically generalized image of a revolutionary epoch and the stage of culmination in the historical destiny of the people.

A mature master and a great artist, Shostakovich completed his enormous work of almost 40 years on a theme whose first sketches he had made as an 18-year-old Conservatory student shaken by the death of the great Soviet leader, Lenin. Shostakovich named the symphony *The Year 1917* and dedicated it to the memory of Lenin. The premiere was held under the direction of Mravinsky in Leningrad on October 1, 1961.

"I've started composing my Thirteenth Symphony. I'd rather call it a vocal-symphonic suite of five parts. I have used for this composition a text by the poet Yevgeny Yevtushenko. On close acquaintance with him, it became clear to me that he is a man of great and, what is most important, thinking talent."

Excerpt from a letter by Dmitry Shostakovich to Vissarion Shebalin, July 1, 1962.

Shostakovich at a concert. Behind him is Aram Khachaturian.

In 1962, Shostakovich married musicologist Irina Supinskaya. Here, the husband and wife are together at an all-Shostakovich recital.

**Shostakovich at the premiere of the Thirteenth Symphony, with poet
Yevgeny Yevtushenko (right) and singer V. Gromadsky (center).**

On December 17, 1962, *Pravda* announced the first performance of Shostakovich's Thirteenth Symphony in Moscow. The next day, the Grand Hall of the Moscow Conservatory was packed to capacity. Musicians of the symphony orchestra of the Moscow Philharmonic, the bass group of the Russian Republican Choir and the Choir of the Gnesin Institute unhurriedly settled themselves on the stage. The audience expected a symphony in which the spoken word would make a comeback, after a long interval, in Shostakovich's music.

The synthesis of the word and music in the Thirteenth Symphony was a direct continuation of the program symphonies *The Year 1905* and *The Year 1917*, in which one could feel under the song material the composer's growing need for a final element lending the utmost concreteness to the narrative for the sake of still greater clarity, precision and populist vividness.

In the new spiral of the evolution of Shostakovich's music, his symphony turned back to poetry. But now the composer was far ahead of the mechanical combination of the two components in the Second and Third symphonies. There it had been a fully independent symphonic "organism" with a percussion vocal-instrumental apotheosis in the finale; here it was the most natural association of music and text literally along all verticals and horizontals: musical intonations sensitively followed the verbal ones, seeking to achieve recitative expressiveness. They actively absorbed elements of vocal sonority and were guided at places by the laws of choral polyphony. They surrounded themselves with supporting voices so common to Russian folk songs and even tried to stay on in the simple and clear constructions of the song couplet.

The five movements of the symphony are based on five different poems of Yevgeny Yevtushenko, which have no connection in plot. The music supplements the text, bringing to light the implication of the verse, argues with it and sums it up, which is possible only for a mature symphonist, and at places rises above the text. The first movement, "Babi Yar," is mournfully tragic; the second scherzo movement is grotesquely sharpened; the third movement, "In a Shop," is lyrically expressive; in the fourth movement, "Fears," the atmosphere is tense and anxious again; and in the fifth, "Career," which is sometimes darkened with ironic intonations, light reigns supreme and the ultimate truth triumphs.

It would seem that the composer clearly indicated the genre of this composition: a vocal-symphonic suite. It is precisely this genre that usually implies a pictorial, outward comparison of different, contrasting genres.

The Thirteen Symphony, however, has a common pivot of meaning which allows this composition to be called precisely a symphony and lends dramaturgical integrity to the whole cycle. This is the lofty spirit of civic devotion denouncing fascism and violence, falsehood and hypocrisy, careerism and unprincipledness, and asserting immutable ethical laws.

138

"... Shostakovich's Thirteenth Symphony is a specimen of a new genre. Let us call it the philosophical-populist genre. Having summed up much of his earlier experience, the composer has produced a qualitatively new fusion of arts. The growing faith in goodness and reason contrary to malice and rabid fanaticism—such is the central idea of the symphony. Indignation at the sight of humanity trampled underfoot, impassioned assertion of the supreme beauty of ethical ideals—these are the qualities of the Thirteenth Symphony that make it a veritable artistic school of justice and humanism."

Sovietskaya Muzyka (Soviet Music), No. 9, 1966.

Twenty days after the first performance of the Thirteenth Symphony, the Muscovites were offered another premiere. On January 8, 1963, the Stanislavsky and Nemirovich-Danchenko Musical Theater staged Shostakovich's opera *Katerina Izmailova* in a new version by the author. Thirty years had passed, and the tragic story of the love and death of a merchant's wife came alive on the same stage. This was a revival of the inspired composition which in its time had opened the list of masterpieces of Soviet classical opera. After some time, *Katerina Izmailova* was revived on the stage of MALEGOT, and in 1964 it stepped over the Soviet border. It was produced in Britain, Yugoslavia, Austria and Hungary ... Shostakovich's second opera began its triumphant tour of the world.

In the meantime, the composer was under the spell of new ideas. He again returned to *Hamlet* and wrote a complex symphonic score for a film under the same name. Its music sounded in solemnly austere unison with the noble and highly philosophical content of Shakespeare's tragedy. During the summer of 1964, he completed his work on the scores of the Ninth and Tenth String Quartets, and before long he finished the last page of his new composition for soloist, choir and orchestra to verses by Yevgeny Yevtushenko, which was entitled *The Execution of Stepan Razin.*

The 17th-century captive insurgent leader, Stepan Razin, a Cossack, fastened to a pillory, beaten up, bleeding and spat upon, is trundled on a cart to Moscow, a white stone city of innumerable church bells, a heavy iron chain strangling his throat and jingling in time with the rumble of the cart over cobblestones. There are crowds watching eagerly on both sides of the road—peasant men and women, servants and petty clerks, merchants and God's fools. They are shouting, jeering and whistling, and the spiteful cry "Stenka Razin going to his death!" is ringing through the streets. Amid the general confusion and excitement, only the voice of the chronicler is dispassionately quiet. Such is the beginning of Shostakovich's composition.

This is not a symphony. Nor is it an oratorio, although the composition called *The Execution of Stepan Razin* contains elements of a symphony and an oratorio and a synthesis of both. This is the central act of the people's drama which needs perhaps only costumes and direct stage action to be called a true opera scene. The composer

"No, I cannot say that I live in the past. I live now, and shall live longer—a hundred years!"

Dmitry and Irina Shostakovich at their country house in Zhukovka, in 1973.

Shostakovich with the world-famous violinist David Oistrakh, to whom he dedicated his Second Violin Concerto. "Oistrakh has performed my concerto several times, and each time with such inspiration and understanding of my intention, and of the ideas and emotions expressed in the music, that I cannot help thinking: if I were a violinist I would try to perform it just like that!"

The composer accepts congratulations after an all-Shostakovich recital.

himself gave the most accurate definition of the genre of "The Execution of Stepan Razin": a vocal-symphonic poem. In it he revealed himself more vividly than anywhere else as heir to Moussorgsky's epic dramatic operas, as heir to what is best in Russian classical music on the theme of the historical past of the people.

This picturesque story, which is concrete to the utmost in some musical details, reproduces the spirit of the ancient Russian legends where the unhurried and outwardly calm narrative only emphasizes the dramatic intensity of events. Thus, the main theme in the poem is the terse, intonationally austere epic melody which leads the entire narrative and pervades the musical fabric like the voice of the chronicler, the stern voice of history itself. It was probably not accidental that Shostakovich made full use in the poem of the timbre of male voices, particularly basses, which evoke direct associations with the voice of Pimen or Dosifei.

The tumultuous scene in which Stepan Razin is brought to Moscow gives way, almost visibly, to the Cossack leader's monologues. One can hear notes of sadness and disappointment and sincere faith in his righteous cause: "I do not repent, I've chosen my fate myself." His aria, which is almost operatic, sounds quietly and simply.

The central scene of the poem is the noisy and bloody scene of Stepan Razin's execution in Red Square, and it is brought to its culmination at the moment when "the crowd in the square understood something and took off their hats." The sudden, dead "silence" of the orchestra is amazingly forceful in its artistic impression, only the strings quietly sounding a transparent and long chord. Shostakovich showed his mastery as a dramatist capable of conveying through the medium of music the psychologically complex moment when the mob suddenly ceases to be a mob and when, in the words of the poem, "Faces grow threateningly in the faceless crowd."

The action nears an end, and the pipe of a God's fool plays with falsely exaggerated cheerfulness while one of the tsar's minions exclaims, "Why are you people standing still? Throw up your hats in the air and dance!" His phrase hangs in a long silence which is then exploded by the laughter of the Cossack's cut-off head. In the finale of the poem, convulsive, restless and tense, the chorus repeats over and over again: "Our fight has not been in vain!"

From reflection to vigorous action is not just one step. And reflection itself is long, contradictory and agonizing. The history of Russia has proved that. The great truth of the poem "The Execution of Stepan Razin" lies in the quiet of its culmination and in the anxiety of its finale. This is the truth of history to which Shostakovich turned once again.

> "... The poem is an optimistic tragedy, a socio-historical tragedy for that matter. This one-movement vocal-symphonic suite is a useful lesson in life as well as in art, as is normal for a truly great composition ..."
>
> S. Slonimsky, *The Triumph of Stepan Razin*, 1965.

Immortality

A Symphony of Supreme Wisdom

On September 25, 1966, Shostakovich would turn sixty. The year was marked by another event of significance for him. On March 29, the composer Dmitry Shostakovich, winner of the Lenin and State prizes and holder of the title of People's Artist of the U.S.S.R., ascended the broad steps of the Kremlin Palace of Congresses carrying a red card in his hand as one of the 5,000 delegates of the 23rd Congress of the CPSU. The Congress lasted for 11 days, and during that time Shostakovich realized with increasing clarity the necessity of his music to the people and just how important the art he had served all his life was.

The time for a great jubilee in Shostakovich's honor was approaching. It was a time for him to review his medals and awards, to inspect his service record and to clean his old uniform, speaking figuratively, before a solemn ceremony.

On May 28, 1966, Shostakovich gave a recital of his works at the Small Hall of the Leningrad Philharmonic. Compositions of a humorous character were the main items on the program. Among them were "Satires" to verses by Sasha Cherny (1960) and the "Five Romances for Voice and Piano" to lyrics from *Crocodile* magazine (1965), which were witty and mischievous portrait sketches to texts from the "Believe It or Not" section, in which the composer caustically mocked small human weaknesses and great human vices.

The concert opened with a work Shostakovich based on the writings of Alexander Pushkin. Its poetical part had been borrowed, with slight alterations, from Pushkin's well-known "Story of a Poet," while the prosaic part was the composer's own contribution. The work was entitled "A preface to my collected compositions and my reflections on this preface."

"I write my verses in a single stroke,
I lend my ear to the angry mob,
Then I abuse the hearing of the world.
And get them published and forgotten."

It was signed: "Dmitry Shostakovich, People's Artist of the U.S.S.R." There were quite a few honorary titles, including First Secretary of the Composers' Union of the Russian Federation and Secretary of the U.S.S.R. Composers' Union, plus many other responsible duties and posts. A man in the true sense of the word, he was capable of mocking himself: "I am not averse to anything that is human."

Dmitry Shostakovich with two of the greatest musicians of his age, David Oistrakh (left) and pianist Sviatoslav Richter (right), brilliant performers of his Second Violin Sonata.

Opposite:
Above: The Beethoven Quartet, "that wonderful ensemble which has made such a contribution to the development of Soviet music," rehearsing at Shostakovich's home. "Personally I have always derived great pleasure from my working association with these talented musicians, and am sincerely grateful for the mastery they have shown in performing my works."
Below: Shostakovich with violinist Dmitry Tziganov of the Beethoven Quartet. "I can remember countless meetings and conversations with this wonderful person and fine musician. . .to whom I am enormously indebted as a composer for his constant attention to my music."

Shostakovich disliked panegyrics and bombastic speeches, the idle talk of windbags. He spoke and wrote simply, without the floweriness of subordinate clauses. A short phrase. Period. Another phrase. Period. He tried to avoid magnificent epithets and superlative statements. It can be seen from his articles, auto-biographical notes and remarks that he very often used the simplest verbs in common usage, such as *wrote, heard, came, finished,* "this is good and this is bad for such and such reason."

Those who were lucky enough to be personally acquainted with Shostakovich unanimously emphasized the main features of his character: restraint, naturalness and simplicity. When the time came for congratulations on his anniversary, for the presentation ceremonies for his third Order of Lenin and the Gold Star of Hero of Socialist Labor, when concerts dedicated to the composer's 60th birthday were held one after another, it was found that he was as shy and awkward before the public as he had always been.

His life, however, was drawing to an end. With every new composition he became ever more clearly aware of the problem of the finale—the finale of human fate and art. With the equanimity that comes with experience, wisdom and long life, he searched for the truth which had attracted the best artistic minds of all mankind—the "truth for all time." Life and death, eternal darkness and the eternal flame of creative spirit, the mysteries of great Time. He ascended to a new level of creative thinking, accessible to few, from which man, his powers and his deeds are clearly visible.

> "He was not engaged in quests of new musical sounds but of a new content. And he was endowed by nature with an ability to find whatever he searched for. . . . The civic element in his art acquired a new spiritual aspect, and music became a still greater revelation than before. In this music one can find answers to the most crucial question as to the meaning of human life and the light of truth. . . ."

Sovietskaya Muzyka (Soviet Music), No. 9, 1974.

The lyrico-philosophical, profoundly ethical element had always been characteristic of Shostakovich's music. In the final period of his life, however, his art was purified of all that was vain and transient and showed its new aspects and its new depths. It was not accidental, therefore, that an echoing of the classics, down to open quotations and reminiscences, became so significant in Shostakovich's music. Reflecting on the great problems of the existence of man, he, a citizen of the twentieth century, conversed with the past as an equal, adopting its artistic experience and asserting his understanding of time.

Shostakovich's musical language became more and more austere and laconic, his thoughts refined to the degree of aphorisms, and his tone of expression more intimate and endearing. He wrote much more chamber music—quartets and romances—now. He felt like speaking in undertones of what was in his heart of hearts.

In the year of his 60th birthday, he completed another two compositions. One of them—the Eleventh Quartet, dedicated to the memory of Vasily Shirinsky, a member of the Beethoven Quartet—is a profoundly lyrical work protesting against the powerful force which sets the fatal limit to life and ruefully recognizing its omnipotence. The other composition—the Second Cello Concerto—was performed on September 25, 1966, on the composer's birthday.

This concerto clearly defined perhaps for the first time the new dramaturgical line that would form the basis for many of Shsotakovich's later works. According to classical laws, the concerto consists of three parts. Nothing in it, however, reminds one of the traditional scheme of imagery and dramaturgy. It has an actively conflictive first part, a quiet and reflective second part and a cheerful and inwardly balanced finale. On the contrary, the circle is reversed. Peace gives way to activity, and activity to peace. There is a supreme artistic meaning in this new solution proposed by Shostakovich.

The first part of the concerto is an austere, epically restrained reflection on life, on eternity, perhaps on fame. It has the concentration of a sage watching the march of time. The second part is life itself, which at times rises to the upper limits of drama and bitter suffering and the death which brings this suffering. The finale in the concluding part returns to wisdom and contemplation, and on its last quiet and lucid pages there is no End but "there is peace and will."

After a few months, the musical public animatedly discussed Shostakovich's new composition: the *Seven Romances* to the verses of Alexander Blok for soprano, violin, cello and piano. Their appearance showed that the Concerto for Cello was not a chance occurrence, that the composer had turned to new themes, new dramaturgy, new means of expression. The press pointed out the amazing harmony between the music and the poems, the recurrence of the idea of the eternal value of life in Shostakovich's art, the exalted and lucid character of the final romances, and the chamber intimacy of their expression.

Particular attention was attracted by the last romance in the cycle, "Music," which is Shotakovich's own kind of ethical and moral credo. His music sang an inspired and solemn hymn to "The Queen of the Universe," a hymn to art to which the artist had given his entire life "through blood, through torture, through death."

In 1967 Shostakovich came up with another instrumental concerto—The Second Concerto for Violin and Orchestra, which he intended to dedicate to David Oistrakh on the occasion of his 60th birthday. It was found, however, that the composer had been mistaken about its date, so a year later he would write a sonata for violin and piano, now with a timely dedication.

"The Sonata literally astounds one from its first audition . . . The performers and listeners are required in the first place to use their intelligence. The composer's

Dmitry and Irina Shostakovich on a walk in Repino, near Leningrad.

Shostakovich at his country house in Zhukovka, in 1973, shortly after his trip to the United States.

Shostakovich sitting for artist Tair Salakhov in his Zhukovka study, in 1974.

reflections are so full of meaning that they cease to be his personal thoughts and assume universal significance.

"The movement of imagery and dramaturgy in the sonata appears to be a kind of spiral in which the finale completing the spiral seems to be called upon to express the continuity of being."

Sovietskaya Muzyka (Soviet Music), No. 9, 1969.

A spiral. The eternal cycle of life with its carefree childhood, the dashing of hopes, the pain and bitterness of losses. And the wise simplicity of the composer's thought. The musical action is completed with a transparent dialogue of a violin and a piano, which endured with philosophical stoicism all the anxiety and tension of the first two movements to acquire peace touched with lucid sorrow in the coda of the finale.

The premiere of the Sonata, held in May 1969, again showed the audience the inimitable world of Shostakovich's art and the inimitably perfect and refined artistic performances of David Oistrakh and Sviatoslav Richter.

Shostakovich spent the summer of 1969 at the composers' retreat in Dilizhan, Armenia, while the Moscow Chamber Orchestra was already rehearsing his next, Fourteenth Symphony.

"... I harbored the idea of my new composition for a long time. This theme first occurred to me as far back as 1962.

"At that time, I orchestrated Moussorgsky's vocal cycle *Songs and Dances of Death* ... *What if I dared to try and continue it,* I thought to myself. But I had no idea as to approach this subject. Now I have again returned to it after hearing a number of great Russian and world classics.

"I was amazed by the great wisdom and artistic expression with which they resolve the 'eternal themes' of love, life and death, although I have my own approach to them in my new symphony."

Dmitry Shostakovich. Excerpt from a *Pravda* interview, April 25, 1969.

His approach was new, indeed, from the viewpoint of the classical interpretation of eternal themes and from the viewpoint of those of his compositions already written. It was the theme of death, unnatural and violent, which cruelly dashes the hopes for happiness, which deprives one of the joy of creative work, and kills young people and lovers. It was not death in the romantic image of fate or the old woman with her merciless scythe but the real and hence particularly sinister image of human injustice, cruelty and murder.

"The collision between the two worlds, the victory of progress over reaction won through suffering and struggle, defense of man against the scourge of fascism, barbarity and cruelty—all that we define as humanism in our day has always constituted the theme and content of literally all the composer's works. And of the Fourteenth Symphony as well. ... These are not simply the dead; these are victims killed by reality, by the system of life.

Shostakovich looked at their fates through the eyes of a Soviet musician, combining classical tradition with his artistic experience."

Nedelya (Week), No. 36, 1973.

Shostakovich wrote another vocal symphony to poems by García Lorca, Guillaume Apollinaire, Wilhelm Kuchelbecker and Rainer Maria Rilke. His choices were not accidental. In the poems of poets of different lands and different periods, different world outlooks and manners of artistic expression, he discerned what they all had in common. This ability of his enabled him to integrate the 11 movements of the symphony into a single, coherent composition without fear of an excessive diversity of images or a looseness of construction.

This common element enabled him to oppose the restrained monologue "De Profundis" (first movement) to the anxious and provocatively frank rhythm of "Malagueña" (second movement), the agonizingly sorrowful, subtle lyricism of "Suicide" (fourth movement) to the undisguised cruelty of "On Guard" (fifth movement), the mockery and malicious sarcasm of "Response of Zaporozhe Cossacks to the Turkish Sultan" (eighth movement) to the delicate nobleness of the message to a friend "Oh Delvig, Delvig" (ninth movement). This common element, despite the obvious autonomy of different parts of the plot and the extremely concrete images of the tragedy, lent Shostakovich's new composition symphonic unity, because every instant of musical reality, many-faced and changeable, revealed the author's lofty ethical-philosophical conception.

The finale of the symphony is profoundly tragic; it is not the enlightenment of a quieted soul but the suffering cry of the whole orchestra. The catharsis seems to be extended behind the limits of the musical whole, but the tragedy at a different level, the level of the eternal themes, remains optimistic. During all the cataclysms of the 20th century, Shostakovich never ceased to talk of the lethal danger of evil, addressing himself to the events of the day (as, for instance, in the Seventh Symphony) and summing up artistically widely different and distant phenomena of reality. In these themes lie the modern character of his interpretation and the wisdom of his Fourteenth Symphony.

"We can find here a dramatic scene of absorbing nervous tension, a mournful elegy, an exalted ode and a grotesque, angry scherzo-march. The main theme runs through all the sections, uniting them . . . It is a tragic theme. Our assessment of the Fourteenth Symphony, however, cannot depend on the fact that it is gloomier than a number of other opuses by the same author. The value of a work of art cannot be defined by measuring the amount of music in major or minor keys, radiant or sad, that it contains. The crux of the matter lies in the 'super-task' . . ."

Sovietskaya Muzyka (Soviet Music), No. 1, 1970.

The composer on stage after an all-Shostakovich recital.

Opposite:

Shostakovich (in a typical posture) and his wife Irina before a 1973 concert in honor of Aram Khachaturian.

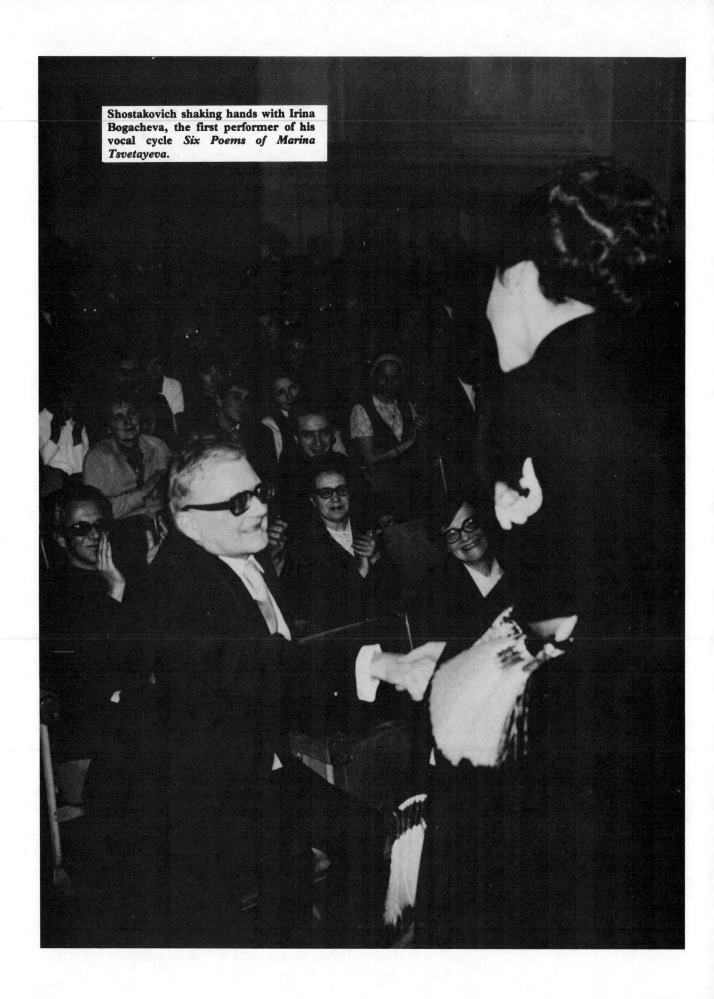

Shostakovich shaking hands with Irina Bogacheva, the first performer of his vocal cycle *Six Poems of Marina Tsvetayeva*.

Cinema. Quartets. Symphony. Vocal Cycles

It so happened that Shostakovich worked on his last film jointly with Grigory Kozintsev, the director of his first film. They had begun in the late 1920s with *New Babylon*, ten years later they worked on the trilogy about Maxim, in 1964 they completed *Hamlet*, and now they were to handle another joint production.

"Dear Dmitry,

"I feel the standard interval is running out (five or maybe seven years), and I am again asking you to write the music for a film. This time it will be *King Lear*. I eagerly hope you will agree."

Excerpt from a letter by Grigory Kozintsev to Dmitry Shostakovich, May 1968.

King Lear. Of course he agreed.

During the long years of their association, the composer and conductor had learned to understand each other without many words. Both heard identically the high and clear tone of Shakespearean tragedies. . . ."To produce *King Lear*, one must have a feeling of grief rather than a sense of moderation. Both of them had this feeling.

On the screen is the abject figure of the jester. Around him are burning ruins, smoke, horses neighing tiredly and clanging soldiers' spears. Someone raises a log and drags it along, leaving behind an irregular furrow in the debris. The jester, walking unsteadily, reaches some half-burned poles and sinks to the ground with his legs bent awkwardly. He throws up his head, and emits a hardly audible high-tone howl through his clenched teeth. Out of habit, his hand feels his clothes, of which nothing but rags remains, and brings a crude home-made instrument—a pipe—to his lips.

The sad pipe of the jester begins and ends the film about the meaning of life, the truth which became clear only after the mind had dimmed, about an 80-year-old king who learns through suffering and grief the measure of all things—what is fair, what is false, what is good and what is evil—and who discovers anew the cruel world in which he lives.

That was a black-and-white film. The means Kozintsev and Shostakovich were seeking were to be the simplest, the barest, the most unsophisticated, so that nothing would interfere with the narrative of the bitter paths of human knowledge but would raise this narrative above time and above history, lending it universal message and appeal. In complete accord with the general plan, Shostakovich's music was simple, sad and unsophisticated.

"Dear Grigory,

"I am sending you the songs of poor Tom . . . Some sadness in performance is necessary . . ."

Excerpt from a letter by Dmitry Shostakovich to Grigory Kozintsev, July 1969.

". . . I like the songs you have sent me very much. They are just what I wanted to hear: pleading village songs. It would be good to avoid wherever possible anything that is loud and solemn and exalted. We need to find intonations that would be humanly sad."

Excerpt from a letter by Grigory Kozintsev to Dmitry Shostakovich, July 1969.

The authors of the film did without a magnificent overture, outwardly brave martial music and life-asserting chords which deafen the listener in the final scenes. The monotonous and sad melody of the pipe, occasionally replaced by a weeping chorus or the musical "voices" of Tom and Cordelia, amazingly support the enormous and complex world of King Lear's tragedy, since it is the voice of Truth, the voice of the author himself, as Grigory Kozintsev put it.

When their work on the film was in full progress, they received the sad news of the death of Vadim Borisovsky, the viola player of the Beethoven quartet. The composer dedicated his Thirteenth Quartet to this wonderful musician, and its premiere was held in December 1970.

This small, one-movement composition speaks of death with noble and quiet sadness. The musical time absorbs the long span of life, and the spiral of human fate is revealed in the spiral completed by the music. The mournful sounds and the sad monologue of the viola, after the protesting and excited retorts of all the four voices, is suddenly followed by a mysterious and fiery dance in which the hollow, unreal strikings of the bow on the sound board only emphasize the cold desert of darkness.

Then the music turns back to the opening theme, and the solo of the viola again develops unhurriedly and sadly, climbing higher and higher and becoming more and more transparent and lucid. This is how the endless thread of time winds its way. That theme of rare beauty seems to be without end, but the ominous strikings suddenly disrupt the thread.

For a few days in the spring of 1971, Shostakovich was busy working at the 24th Congress of the CPSU. The Congress discussed the problems of the next Five-Year Plan, heard reports and resolutions, discussed amendments in the rules of the Communist Party, and drafted the Peace program. It was matter-of-fact, regular work of the party and government, and Shostakovich, as a deputy of the U.S.S.R. Supreme Soviet since 1962, had always taken an active part. Sometime later he would be decorated with the Order of the October Revolution in recognition of his services to the state.

In the autumn of the same year, it became known that Shostakovich had completed his next, Fifteenth Symphony and that the Grand Symphony Orchestra of the U.S.S.R. Radio and TV Broadcasting Service had already started to rehearse it. The premiere of the symphony was being prepared by Maxim Shostakovich, who would conduct the performance of his father's new composition for the first time on January 8, 1972.

> "The symphony was written in the summer of 1971. I worked upon it very hard but rather quickly, roughly for two months. I feel quite excited before the premiere . . . It is always hard to comment on one's own compositions, but it will certainly be a pleasure for me to know that the audience has received my Fifteenth Symphony favorably."

> Dmitry Shostakovich. Excerpt from *Vechernyaya Moskva (Moscow Evening News)* interview January 8, 1972.

The listeners were presented with an instrumental drama. The composer had again felt the need to return to pure symphonic music, to the classically austere composition in four movements, in which there were no words but there was the familiar spontaneity of non-program symphonic music capable of resolving the most profound and complex themes of life.

The symphony proved laconic and very lyrical, and critics immediately sensed a resemblance, an almost imperceptible link of this symphony to the Ninth, which had created such a sensation at one time. This restless composer always in search of innovation again proposed a new solution to the cycle. Not for an entertaining and carefree play with classical forms, which he could certainly afford, but in response to some inner voice which dictated precisely such a solution.

The symphony painted in four movements what seemed two similar circles, and in each of them the collision of life and death was presented in its own way.

Two crystal clear and joyful strikes of a bell open the first movement of the symphony. A flute begins to sing a simple and light melody, and now different groups of instruments whirl and interrupt one another in a vigorous and joyous dancing motion; there is a merry fuss and noise and a scuffle without malice here and there. This is either a galop or a polka danced by children hopping along. There is no grotesque or even a hint of irony, but gentleness and care, as though a recollection of the effervescent fantasy, spontaneity and radiance of the wonderful time of childhood. The general merriment is invaded by the summoning voices of two trumpets in which a sophisticated listener will immediately recognize an excerpt from Rossini's "William Tell"—swift, joyful and radiant music. Is it a scherzo? Of course. The transparent and carefree world of youth or, perhaps, of a kind fairy tale, for which everyone feels affection and attachment as long as he lives.

The chorale opening the second movement of the symphony is austere and mournful. The tone of the monologues pronounced in turn by the cello, the violin, the flutes or the trombone is serious and restrained. The sounds are mournful, the culminations are tense, and the endings of phrases are full of grief.

The third movement opens a new circle again at the light pace of a scherzo, which, however, is far more anxious and excited than the first. This is a real world, a complex and grave world, where a good-natured joke turns into glum sarcasm and where the nobleness of spirit at times evokes nothing but a condescending smile.

And then the finale. Here everything is also quite obvious, quite real, and called by its own name. The last movement opens with a brief, questioning intonation followed by a long series of associations—the theme of fate from Wagner's *Der Ring des Nibelungen*, a kind of theme-symbol of the romantic 19th century, always seeking, always unsatisfied, always aspiring toward a beautiful but, alas, unattainable ideal. The question was put to Time and to Eternity.

The elegiac, melodious theme in Russian style coming on after a long pause is frail and helpless like a child. Its image is sad. The frailness and delicacy of this theme are strikingly obvious when they are threatened by the deadly march of the second melody, easily recognizable as the theme of the enemy invasion from the Leningrad Symphony. The heroes are named, and the mournful monologues of the second movement, deprived of any personification whatsoever, give place in the finale to two extremely concrete images.

Their juxtaposition and simultaneous conduction seems unnatural since the difference between them is much too glaring—white and black, living and dead, high and low. It is necessary to pass through a long and painful ascent toward the culmination, to live through the culmination itself, to appreciate in full the staunchness and courage of the frail motif which appeared after the deepest despair and grief, after the question put to Time again and again.

There follows the coda of the finale and simultaneously the coda of the symphony as a whole. Images from the preceding movements flash and gradually dissolve in it, the sounding of the orchestra becomes clearer and more transparent, and now only the bells, the celesta, the xylophone and the triangle emit crystal-clear and lucid sounds on the background of the airy and transparent chord of the strings endlessly extended in time. The Fifteenth Symphony ends amid complete silence.

"What in this music excites us most of all? Why is the audience listening to it so tensely and avidly? Everyone reflects on the purpose of his life at least once in a lifetime; everyone is destined to live through the pain of irretrievable losses and to try to find courage in the face of the inevitable. Over the years, we learn to value in a new way the warmth of a friendly smile, the wisdom of a simple tune, the subdued beauty of natural scenery, and the heartfelt devotion of the near and dear ones."

Ibid., January 11, 1972.

The year 1973 enriched the list of Shostakovich's compositions with two new chamber opuses. The composer dedicated his Fourteenth Quartet, music of exalted and inspired beauty, to the memory of Sergei Shirinsky, the cellist of the Beethoven Quartet. The same beauty, the same austerity and natural simplicity, was opened to listeners of Marina Tsvetayeva's Six Poems for contralto and piano.

On November 15, 1974, Shostakovich's Fifteenth Quartet was premiered in Leningrad. In this composition he reached the summits of artistic revelation.

> "Those who were fortunate to attend the premiere were literally spellbound . . . no other words would better define the feelings of the listeners. Again and again Shostakovich turns to a theme no great artist will ignore: the meaning of life. In his wise enlightenment, the author has realized the inevitable dramatic dialectics of life and death, death and immortality. The power of untainted spiritual beauty created by man reigns supreme over everything else in the quartet."
>
> *Vecherny Leningrad (Leningrad Evening News)*, November 19, 1974.

In the days of the premiere of the Fifteenth Quartet, Shostakovich revealed his short-term creative plans almost by accident, in a fleeting newspaper interview. He was already collecting material for a composition dedicated to the 30th anniversary of Soviet victory in World War II.

> "I have a feeling that three decades have not yet passed and that everything happened only yesterday. Although I don't like making promises, I can say that I am working on a new symphonic composition commemorating the historic date of our victory. Of course, it is too early to offer anything, nor do I know anything about Eugene Mravinsky's creative plans. But I would like my work to be first performed in Leningrad."
>
> Dmitry Shostakovich. Excerpt from a *Vecherny Leningrad (Leningrad Evening News)* interview, November 15, 1974.

Unfortunately, this conception failed to be translated into reality. Other plans already embodied in music and committed to paper in the composer's quick, angular handwriting impatiently waited for their own premieres.

Literally a week after the sensational success of the Fifteenth Quartet, the premiere of Shostakovich's vocal suite for bass and piano based on Michelangelo's poetry was held in Leningrad. The composer tended toward the most intimate and frank revelations, ever greater transparency and simplicity of musical language, and searched for the means capable of expressing the most delicate emotions. Now he turned to the poetry of the Renaissance, for which the moral perfection of man was the criterion of all things.

"This man is a compatriot of not only the Italians; he belongs to all nations. Such is the phenomenon of Michaelangelo. His poetry attracts one by its profound philosophical thoughts, lofty humanism and brilliant judgments on art and love. My suite for bass and piano is based on eight sonnets and three poems by Michelangelo. Here there is lyricism and drama and two delighted panegyrics devoted to Dante. I have myself given titles to all the songs or romances, since the author did not give them names; but they are suggested by the content of his poems."

Dmitry Shostakovich. Excerpt from *Leningradskaya Pravda* interview, December 24, 1974.

The vocal suite united 11 poems on a variety of themes, just as the Fourteenth Symphony had been based on different poems. "Truth," "Morning," "Love," "Parting," "Anger," "Dante," "Fugitive," "Art," "Night," "Death," "Immortality"—11 poems like milestones marking the main stages in human life. Their simple and calm sequence revealed the very same plain truth to the composer. Nothing in Shostakovich's music was superfluous, affected or incidental; the confident and terse strokes of a chisel, the salience of a bas-relief, the austere expressiveness of stone.

The next opus was *The Four Poems of Captain Lebyadkin* (from Dostoyevsky's *Devils*) as a direct extension of the characteristically sharp and grotesque "Satires" to a text by Sasha Cherny, romances from *Crocodile* magazine. *The Four Poems* were not a "relaxation" after the majestic cycle of Michelangelo but a complete and profound manifestation of creativity—multiform, changeable and wise.

After the two premieres in Leningrad, he went with special pleasure to Moscow, where the Chamber Musical Theater staged his first opera, *The Nose*, restored in the autumn of 1974 by its company under the guidance of its music director and conductor, Boris Pokrovsky.

"Dmitry Shostakovich dreamed of seeing the opera of his youth performed again in Russia. I became keenly aware of that at a performance of *The Nose* in Berlin. Then Shostakovich expressed his warm thanks to the company for the production, lavishing praise on its members in words of delight, but his eyes were sad. He never praised us like that and even withheld his praise altogether, but he worked with us, and his eyes were kind and happy."

Boris Pokrovsky, *Liberation From Bias*, 1976.

Before every next performance of *The Nose* at the Chamber Musical Theater on Leningradsky Avenue, admirers swarming in front of the building asked imploringly for an extra ticket and the lucky ones packed the cramped theater hall to capacity. The tom-tom thumped the first note of the score, a military drum trilled like a bird, and the story of a "fantastic accident" with Major Kovalev's nose started at a brisk pace to begin a second life of "the first original opera composed in Soviet territory by a Soviet composer." (Ivan Sollertinsky).

Opus 147, and the Last

Between May 5 and 13, 1975, Moscow was the site of the Moscow Stars art festival. During this annual musical event, *The Four Poems of Captain Lebyadkin* were played for the first time. That was the last premiere attended by Shostakovich.

On June 2, the composer came to Leningrad to listen to a new symphony by Revol Bunin, a pupil of his. On June 6, the newspaper *Sovietskaya Kultura* published Shostakovich's article "A Company of Wonderful Musicians" about the Taneyev company, the first performers of his Fifteenth Quartet. Little by little, material was collected for a composition commemorating the 30th anniversary of victory in World War II, and he was already at work composing the Sonata for Viola and Piano dedicated to Fedor Druzhinin, the viola player who had replaced Vadim Borisovsky in the Beethoven Quartet.

As usual, Shostakovich had fully determined the plan of his new composition before he committed it to paper. He visualized the first part of the sonata as something "like a novella." The second part was to be a scherzo. The finale of the sonata, adagio, was dedicated to the "memory of the great composer, Beethoven." On the morning of June 25, 1975, the composer made the first few sketches of his new composition.

> ". . . On September 25, 1975, which was his birthday (he would have been 69 on that day), the composer's friends assembled in his apartment after a concert where his Fourteenth Symphony—about death—was played. Two wonderful musicians—the viola player Fedor Druzhinin, to whom the sonata was dedicated, and the pianist Mikhail Muntyan—played it for us for the first time. This is a sonata about life and about the glory of life. Its third, and last, movement for its tense and vigorous lyricism is perhaps without parallel in all of Shostakovich's heritage."

Leo Arnstam, *The Music of the Heroic,* 1977.

Shostakovich did not live to hear his new compositions. His friends dedicated their meeting on September 25 to his memory. The Fourteenth Symphony, the Fifteenth Quartet, the Suite for Bass and Piano to poems by Michelangelo, which opened the new season in the concert halls, were also played in commemoration of the composer. Fedor Druzhinin and Mikhail Muntyan **were** rehearsing the Sonata for Viola and Piano for its first public performance to honor his memory.

The premiere was held in the Small Hall of the Leningrad Philharmonic, named after Glinka, on October 1, which had been proclaimed as the first International Music Day by UNESCO's International Musical Council. Shostakovich's permanent seat in the fifth row was covered with flowers.

On that morning in June, however, all this was yet to happen. Shostakovich was in a Moscow hospital ward surrounded with care and attention by medical personnel. He had a short conversation with Druzhnin by phone, and now the first nervous lines of Opus 147 hastily appeared on music paper.

"Dear Kristof,

I thank you for your letter and for remembering me . . . Now I am in a hospital. I have some trouble with my heart and lungs. I can write with my right hand with great difficulty. Although it was hard work, I wrote the Sonata for Viola and Piano."

Excerpt from a letter by Dmitry Shostakovich to Kristof Meyer, July, 1975.

The Sonata for Viola completed the triad of Shostakovich's chamber works for string instruments. The Cello Sonata appeared in 1934, the Violin Sonata in 1969, and now it was the Viola Sonata. The Viola Sonata was a composition for an instrument which has perhaps the warmest and most velvety timbre of all, without the resonance of the cello and without the open sounding of the high registers of the violin. This is a voice of trust and frankness.

The first part of the sonata is dramatically excited, the hollow sounds of the viola falling into space drily and cautiously, and the piano interrupting it in a voice which is also sharp, dry and excited. This is a serious conversation, and its end does not dispel the atmosphere of anxiety but, on the contrary, accentuates the sombre, almost grievous, intonations.

The second part switches the mind to scherzo dancing images, which, however, are devoid of complete carelessness and the holiday spirit of merriment. The anxious tone and internal tension are only emphasized by the short bursts of the piano and the resolute, almost declarative monologues of the viola. Anxiety, now open, now secret, is both in the world of reflection and in the world of action.

In the concluding adagio, the viola speaks in a quiet voice free from any constraint, in which all possible intonations of the human voice are audible. This is impassioned, pathetic speech rising to the degree of Weltschmerz and resolving in lucid tranquility only to rise to high passion again. Most amazing of all is the background which supports and carefully sustains this lonely and proud speech. The incessant transparent figurations of the piano distinctly echo the first, slow part of Beethoven's Moonlight Sonata. A long series of associations come to life: heroic spirit, lofty patriotism, the "objective" motivation of the subtlest feelings, pure and exalted lyricism in which the notion of self is inseparable from the notion of the universe. Everything is proportionate, perfect and governed by the simple, wise and eternal laws of nature.

"... This finale is precisely the credo of the artist who discarded all that is vain and trifling. In all of the last compositions of Shostakovich, the motif of departure from life is certainly present, and sorrow is easily discerned. Nevertheless, in this sonata the motif of goodness, love and all-conquering faith in life relegates everything else to the background. One has the impression that some invisible architect has lent Shostakovich's whole life and art an inimitable coherent form. Perhaps his last composition could not have been different ..."

Literaturnaya Gazeta (Literary Gazette), September 7, 1977.

Beside the two lines marking the end of the sonata, the composer wrote: "D. Shostakovich July 5, 1975." On the same day, the 64 pages of the thoroughly verified manuscript were sent to the copyists and were returned after a month for final verification. On August 6, the Sonata for Viola and Piano was handed over to Fedor Druzhinin.

On August 9, 1975, Dmitry Shostakovich passed away.

"... My name is Musin. My profession is a doctor. I have learned of Dmitry Shostakovich's death today, and I deem it my duty to write this letter. Year after year, from one composition to another, I learned the music of Shostakovich, and now I am obliged to say that I love this music, and everything it speaks of has always moved me. Its most impressive quality, to my mind, is its profound humaneness."

– E. Musin, the city of Ufa.

"... Is Shostakovich difficult to understand? Yes. But this is forgotton as soon as one becomes familiar with his music. Of course, he is unlike Tchaikovsky, just as Mayakovsky is unlike Nekrasov. The harmony is more complex; the contrasts are more striking. My favorite is the Leningrad Symphony. I cannot forget the blockade and the ordeal of our evacuation across Lake Ladoga."

– L. Solovyova, Zara Kommunisma State Farm, Moscow Region.

"... He is wise not only in his compositions, his acts and his words but also in his outlook. His wisdom is simple but it is the profound wisdom of the people which does not strike the eye."

– T. Uralov,
a shipyard worker, the city of Nikolayev.

"... One is amazed by broad range of Shostakovich's music. He is an unexcelled jack-of-all-trades."

– Y. Shipitsyn,
a carpenter, the city of Irkutsk.

"... He helps one to appreciate the joy of life, struggle and construction. He gives one the happiness of association with a world of beauty and suspense. It is the world of great music."

– V. Lyulin, the city of Vladimir.

"Who can stop the music I have thought of from coming out?. . . So long as I have a pencil and paper, it would be impossible."

"Shostakovich's music is inimitable and can be easily recognized from a few notes even if it is a passage from an unfamiliar work. His musical language is austere and pure and is alien to embellishment."
— T. and A. Vernigora,
the town of Usolye-Sibirskoye,
Irkutsk Region.

". . . In the Seventh Symphony the composer has brilliantly portrayed the theme of the invasion. I am sure that this music is worth many volumes describing the horrors of fascism."
— V. Buzinovsky, an engineer,
Sverdlovsk.

". . . The death of Dmitry Shostakovich is tragic news for all people who love music. He is the most impressive, the most brilliant composer I know."
— V. Armashev, a plasterer and
electrician, a veteran of two Komsomol shock
construction projects.

". . . On May 12, 1926, my [First] Symphony was performed under the baton of Nikolai Malko in the Philharmonic hall . . . The success and good playing of the symphony inspired me with confidence and hope. I will work without respite in the field of music, and I pledge to devote all my life to it."
— Dmitry Shostakovich, *A Life Story,* June 16, 1926.

One of the last pictures of Dmitry Shostakovich (June 1975).

Index

(Page numbers in *italics* refer to illustrations.)